To Derek —

I hope Wilshire brings lots
of fun thoughts @ inspiration.
Forever THE LIGHT!

Russ
PR'05

*also by*
Russell Cutts

Blackbird Dreams

Archaeogeophysical Detection and
Mapping of Cherokee Village Patterning
at the Chattooga Town  Historic Site
(38[oc]18), South Carolina

# WILD FIRE

## fire making art

## Russell Cutts

with illustrations by Christina Gordon

WildFire–Fire Making Art

Illustrations © 2004 by Christina Gordon/ North Georgia Art
Cover design © 2004 Russell Cutts, with Mike Hope/ FXArcane and
Christina Gordon/North Georgia Art
Book design and layout by Russell Cutts and Christina Gordon
Printed in the United States of America
First published as a paperback in 2004
Photo credits include Betty Frady, Russell Cutts, Christina Gordon, Mike
Hope, NASA/Space Telescope Center, David Wescott
No names have been changed to protect identities.

Feel free to engage in the practice of ancient lifeways.
But try it before you judge it. For more information about literature from The Wyldecraft Co. or Russ Cutts, write to 722 Shoal Creek Road, Canton, Georgia 30114.

www.wyldecraft.com
www.northgeorgiaart.com
www.earthskills.net
www.primitive.org

ISBN 0-972-6839-1-7
First Edition

This work is dedicated to the remembrance
of family and friends–ancestors all in
spirit or flesh–whose departure has
left our world with a touch of sorrow,
if not for a spark of wisdom and joy, too;

And with special gratitude, thanks to
the Boy Scouts of America.

# Contents

# Acknowledgments

"Never, never, never give up."
—Winston Churchill

**Thanks** go to my parents for their love that is so strong. Although I believe that *unconditional love* is nefariously beyond humanity—misunderstood and possibly misused besides—I readily admit that genuine loving parents are invaluable. May grace honor your efforts and dedication and integrity with *the real thing*.

So many people have extended their encouragement to my writing. Without Christina Gordon this project would not have come to completion. I cannot thank you enough. Thanks to the "four-horsemen" (now inevitably something akin to the "bunch-of-horsemen"). You guys always keep me honest and athough I bemoan that appellation assigned us in high school, if it must be...then I get to be Pestilence. Thanks to Clare Fulkes Adams for pre-reading the entire document in *one day* and saying, "That was really fun!" Mike Hope, the cover design turned out *kewl*. Thanks to NASA and the Space Telescope Center for the Hubble Images used to create that cover. Thanks to Alexa and

Jesse Ihns, in fact *all* of my students who regularly teach me of humility, among other things; your enthusiasm for learning keeps me feeling young.

I owe a real debt to my friends and mentors–family really–in the 'earthskills community.' Alphabetically: Dick Baugh, Robin Blankenship, Frank and Laurie Chambless, Judson Conway and his brother–the last American *man*–Eustace Conway, Richard Cleveland, "Ranger" Doug Elliott, Jeff Gottlieb, Keith Grenoble, David Holladay, Ted "Hawk" Hurst, R. Scott Jones, Norm Kidder, Ben Kirkland, Mac Maness, John and Geri MacPherson, Ron Macy, Matt Richards, Jim Riggs (what was I thinking? *Of course you can wear braintan shorts on a airplane!*), Preston and Kathleen Roberts, Bob Slack Jr., Valarie Spratlin, Steven "Snow Bear" Taylor, Mark Warren, Steve Watts, David Wescott, Darry Wood, and *one other guy whose name I can't remember*; these people–there are masters among them–gave some of their time to me. So many others have provided companionship and encouragement as well. And still others, whom I've not yet met, but whose work influenced mine, include Scott Kuipers and Ken Wee, Richard Jamison, of course Tom Brown, Jr., and the indubitable Larry Dean Olsen–what a genuine pleasure it was to spend an afternoon in conversation with you, Mr. Olsen.

And so having recognized some colleagues who respect and preserve our ancestral ways, I must add that it is *in honor of our ancestors* that I write this book. Truly expressed, our intrepid predecessors had a great will to live. And although we euphemistically make statements such as "the road to Hell is paved with good intentions," it strikes me as callously unfair to lump human creativity, imagination, care, diligence, nurturance and inventiveness into such a cynical sentence.

Surely each of us can identify with the desire to caretake those we love, and it is without a shadow of a doubt that I can state that such is the underlying movement–emotion–giving foundation to the amazing phenomenon that fire has forged in us. Oppenheimer expressed his clear grief that his understanding of physics yielded such a sick eventuality as witnessed in the holocaust of Hiroshima and Nagasaki. Of course, it will be forever unknown how many more would have perished via human exertion of fire-power in the resolution of global war had those bombs not shocked both sides into a new paradigm.

Nevertheless, our ancestors and our selves share the common fate of existing as beings beholden to the righteousness of fire–its powers of judgement, destruction and rejuvenation. Regardless of semantics, human beings owe their existence–physically, mentally, emotionally and spiritually–to the illimitably pure dynamism of Life known as Fire.

And so, with ignorantly insufficient humility, I nonetheless acknowledge above all the Mystery of Ultimate Reality. Such power, such amazing creativity, such incredibly terrifying beauty radiates!

# WILD FIRE

fire making art

# Introduction

"Imagination is the elixir of life."
—P.T. Barnum

As a youth I entered the Scouting movement. My father is an Eagle Scout, and my three older brothers (no sisters) all joined a local Boy Scout Troop (241). One brother soon developed a more profound interest in music which superseded Scouting. On the other hand, two of my brothers and I maintained enough zeal to finish Eagle rank. So it is the kind of nuclear family that generates four Eagle Scouts that set the stage for my life of "naturalism."

This is not necessarily the outcome of such a family. Much of modern Scouting has become what I term "digitized." Now, even though ancient earthskills were the primal digital scientific technologies, the colloquial use of the term *digital* gives clear implication to being *computerized*. Computerized is such a silly term. Computers—blobs of petroleum and wire using electricity to harness the virtual storage capacity of silica—don't actually *do* much of anything. Really they do only what they are told, usually by human digits on a keyboard.

How truly strange we humans are.

Well, even though the Scouting of the Natural World may be heading the way of the Ivory-billed Woodpecker–that is to say pretty damn rare, if not extinct already–it is with sincere loving challenge that I give back what Scouting *never gave to me*. Two-stick Fires.

For all of their hubristic blustering, neither the Boy Scout Handbook or Scouting individuals revealed to me the mystery of mastery of rubbing two sticks to generate fire. But better still, and so much more importantly, Scouting *did* instill in me the confidence of *I can do it!* I believe that understanding our ancient lifeways expands the joy in our modern human condition. Therefore I believe that all scouts–indeed *everyone*–will find great benefit in exploring human antiquity. The benefits are not tied to a return to Stone Age living–heavens no!, and completely impractical!–rather our sense of belonging, appreciation, accomplishment and triumph become honed by *facts*, not teetering at the whim of pretense. We do not know what will befall the human race, but we can surely gain ever greater awareness of how we've come this far.

(Let me also make clear that although some of the above states that I've encountered some blustery and spitefully proud Scouters–which I must sadly include myself–my actual Scoutmaster was and is one of the most humble and sincere men I have ever met. And although not so humble, my Assistant Scoutmaster is one of the most brilliant and competent men I know. As well, each of us is an individual with personal preferences that will dictate not only what we learn but how we teach. There are many in Scouting who practice primitive technologies. There are vastly more in Scouting that sadly–and flagrantly–lie about their accomplishments, be they primitive skills or otherwise.)

I began teaching myself the miracle of friction fire around the age of thirteen or fourteen. It might have been a bit sooner, in that one never knows when an addiction begins. I was definitely bitten by the firebug. I liked to be the one who started our campfires. I prided myself on my one-match competition fires that "burned the victory string first." I picked up the skill of flint and steel (and not only the Bic type!), with charred-cloth and tinderbundle. I learned what made good tinder and the catching beauty of heartpine–"fatlighter." I loved it when morning came and I could rekindle the flames for breakfast from the coals of dinner's hearth. Candles mesmerized me. Watching a candle flame leap across the smoke trail from another candle just extinguished–this struck my curiosity as a deliberate enticement to ponder the mystery enflamed.

It was natural, then, that I should be caught by the assertion in the Boy Scout Handbook that–in an emergency–a person could make a fire by rubbing two sticks together. My handbook, and every one I've ever seen since–was shamefully skimpy on the details. This would not be apparent to the professional Scouters who are charged with editting subsequent editions of "the book." How *could* they know that the subtleties of friction fire were basically *absent* from their "bible"? There is great likelihood that few–if any–of those executives ever succeeded in making fire this way...heck, "*where there's smoke, there's fire, right?*"

Anyone who has become an art-*ist* in the primitive fire arts knows that this sad statement is testament to...blustery. There is no better teacher than experience, no better way to learn than to do, and no quicker way to know someone's flubbing than to have flubbed that way yourself!

So my youthful exuberance faded into a semblance of maturity. Making fire by twirling two sticks together (while though related to, is not quite as difficult as rocket science) is a

**4**

challenge at best. There are terribly many variables that affect the novice, many of which will continue to beset the accomplished! Beyond skill and experience, there will always remain material incompetency, weather conditions, personal wherewithal (e.g.–an injury?), and so forth. I try to always remember these things when I see the incredulity so evident on faces when–during the course of my normal work–these techniques are demonstrated so efficaciously as to have embers in 10 seconds and flames in perhaps thirty. Their attention is so absorbed by the business at hand–wow! smoke so fast? "I thought it would take so much longer!" "Can I try that?"–that they inescapably miss the most important issue: practice *approaches* perfect. No amount of practice allows anyone–*anyone*–to overcome the unpredictability of chaos. The mark of the *true* master is humility.

Through the course of failure I began to learn success. At first fires were by no means guaranteed, much less expected. Smoke was no problem, but getting that ember to ignite in that dust pile was onerous and frustrating! I experimented with many different types of wood, having heard that "only certain types of wood will work." (technically bogus, practically true) I created and used and wore out fire kit after fire kit, never achieving anywhere near what I would call mastery–predictability. Once, one of my close friends and mentors (you know who you are, Mr. "Who, Me?...Noooooo! Jones") assisted my fire development by "loaning" me his "number one, works like a charm, kit." Well, this "easy-kit"–with its ludicrous spindle of some flagrantly dense hardwood–sure carried the novice (that would be me) to a new level. After days of backbreaking effort, voluminous smoke, blood, sweat and tears, my friend came to "review my progress." I still remember, vividly, my parents (visiting me at college) and I, outside my residence, undergoing the tutelage of my colleague. With some humor he replaced the practically fossilized hardwood

5

spindle with yucca–or maybe it was cedar or basswood, you get my drift–and Shazaam! With his well-intentioned duplicity, he had demonstrated something far more subtle than even the transmogrification of matter into energy: the artistry of skill. Style. Panache. Confidence born not of arrogance, but of the humility of experience.

Nevertheless, even with the hit-and-miss success prior to this pivotal lesson, I was always courageous (foolhardy?) enough to demonstrate "the method"–if not the success–of friction fire-starting to group after group of schoolkids, church gatherings, recreation programs and so on. I even was able to finish college and graduate school in large part through the (granted not excessive) income generated from "earthskills presentations." If the word *professional* can be ascribed upon the reciept of payment for services rendered, then I became a professional practicing primitive at the age of seventeen! Well, as a teen I'm absolutely certain that my "skills" mentors chuckled mightily at the "still wet-behind-the-ears upstart" (who still talks too much).

Thousands of campfires later those mentors are like family, and the work of earthskills has become like a mission of destiny so natural to me that the entirety of our human condition seems writ large in the script of the Tool. Man–the eminent toolmaker. Fire–his inevitable companion. Human culture–a legacy of inventive creativity never truly embodying pure imagination...always founded in what has come before. The very questions giving impetus to the searching of science emanating from the wellspring of our past. A consciousness whose collective voice resounds of one primal gestalt: "how?" "why?" "whereforth springs such Mystery?"

The Tree of Knowledge–and its fruits of good and evil–merely the flowering bloom from the tangled garden of human thought. Thoughts whose innocence cannot suffice as reparation for the accidental trials and errors. Fire's grandiose aloofness illuminates–simultaneously–human ignorance and brilliance. Truly, we are *Children* of Light.

So now, years later, I still chase dreams of fire. I still entertain the masses with my exuberant but compassionate pyromania. Incessantly I am drawn to fire. From the need of comfort to the electricity fueling my "blob of petroleum, wire and silica" to the symbolism of hate–and better yet, love; I still rely on fire. I relish and languish in my addiction to it.

I also hope to improve (my still not excessive) income through using it yet again: *WildFire–Fire Making Art.* This volume began through the neverending encouragement of not only family and friends, but amazingly through the insistence of strangers. For...hmmm? around 15 years I have traveled, working to educate about human antiquity. Fire–being central to this theme–always serves as a touchstone for skill after skill, tool after tool, craft after craft. And with upwards of 2,000 fires twirled each year (this figure initially struck me as tacitly impossible. Regardless, after refiguring it many times, it seems loosely accurate. Funny too, on retrospect, is that I'm *sure* that I know some folks who put me to shame), there have been many tens of thousands of observers to this amazing human accomplishment. Time after time these random individuals of the public took it upon themselves to say: "you know, guy, you have a really bizarre but fun way with words...and boy, do you know how to explain fire! You should *write a book!*"

Well, it may be that *WildFire* was not exactly what they had in mind...but it became what my mind had to offer.

Still, I wonder, "*how* much more *don't* I know?"

A good walker leaves no tracks;
A good speaker makes no slips;
A good reckoner needs no tally;
A good door needs no lock,
Yet no one can open it.
Good binding requires no knots,
Yet no one can loosen it.

Therefore the sage takes care of all men
And abandons no one.
He takes care of all things
And abandons nothing.

This is called "following the Light."

What is a good man?
A teacher of a bad man.
What is a bad man?
A good man's charge.
If the teacher is not respected,
And the student not cared for,
Confusion will arise, however clever one is.
This is the crux of mystery.

Lao Tsu, *Tao Te Ching*, 27

# Who Knows the First Fire?

Do not put out the Spirit's fire. Do not
treat prophecies with contempt. Test everything.
Hold onto good, discard all evil.
I Thessalonians 5: 19-22

Sunshine morningly streamed into the copse of
trees hunkered alongside the rock outcropping while he sat
industriously grinding on his *whoomphra*. A nice piece of limb was
slowly being converted into his favorite tool—by rubbing the dead
limb on a convenient stone slab he was able to shape the short
stick to suit his needs. Already accomplished was the general
length and body shape, about half his height and cross-section
mimicking the horizon—curved at a distance but flat under his
feet. One side of the stick was gently arching, the bottom flat
from the split. One end was left slightly bulbous, while the other
had been grindingly tapered to a flat, blade like style. His *whoomphra*—he called it that because that was its noise when he swung
it—was good for digging roots, grubs, termites, honey and other
things. He also chopped into the occasional carcass and cracked
open bones. The whoomphra flew fairly straight and was good to
keep other animals away from his scavenges... and every now and
then he hit something. He thought a lot about hitting something.

As he finished his touch-ups on the finely tapered end, he thought he'd wait out the midday heat in the shade of the rocks and scrub. Besides the added benefit of tepid pockets of water tucked in the shaded rocks, there were a couple of split-fallen tree trunks that might have grubs. Perhaps he'd steadily work on hardening the blade end by rubbing on wood, instead of rock, as the wood is softer and polishes rather than grinds. As he worked on rubbing his whoomphra against the fallen tree to polish and harden it, he began to think about the smoky smell from yesterday. The wind had brought the mouth watering flavor of smoke and he was considering foraging that direction to see if he might find some dead animals. Fire always left dead animals—he just had to find them first and protect them while he got a good meal. Looking up to the distance, he let his mind wander to the flavor of fired meat...and sub-consciously rubbed more briskly in anticipation. Not knowing that his mind had made up itself, he communicated a subtle urgency in the task at hand—rubbing the wooden blade to a hard edge—and sped up to finish and get on his way. As the insinuating awareness of his decision became manifest, he surprised himself by salivating once more. Oddly, there was not much breeze. Perhaps just enough wind to waft the wildfire fumes again?

While stridently working to finish and be on his way, in pleased bemusement he glanced to assess his handiwork...and was intrigued by ephemeral wisps of smoke rising from his whoomphra! Or the fallen tree, one.... He stopped momentarily to examine the blade—it wasn't polished, it was...blackened! Without absolute comprehension, but with some trepidatious excitement, he resumed rubbing his whoomphra in the same groove...and was quickly rewarded with fumes, then faint drafts of light smoke...and then nothing as a small breeze lifted his smoke away. Angrily confused—he wanted more smoke—he stroked furiously against the dried log, immediately producing much more smoke. In moments his muscles fatigued, and he paused, exertion overpowering his vagrant curiosity. The whoomphra blade was long completed. He was wasting energy anyway.

As he jumped astride the log to survey the landscape and stretch his tired back and shoulders, he felt the cool breeze ease. He smelled smoke again. Looking down, he could see a greasy yellow colored smoke—almost like the greasy smoke of a prairie fire—alighting from the dead tree. Bending down, with the sunlight briefly sliding behind shadowed leaf, his stomach churned and his mind raced as he made out a reddish, glowing, eerie ember—smoldering with a baleful gaze that made the hair on his arms rise in warning, and mystery....

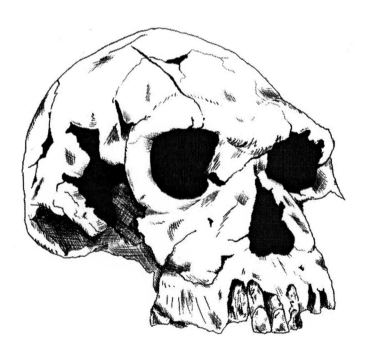

# What is Fire?

*Cogito, ergo sum.* I think, therefore I am.
—Rene Descartes

**What** is fire?

Excellent question. Thanks for asking. What is *your* answer?

*Fire* is a *word* that describes one of the earliest tools known to humans. I say this because fire-as-tool is undeniably one of the principle requirements of defining humanity. If a "people" don't control and use fire, we don't think of them as people, or human. There are no non-fire people.

We're weird that way. We place arbitrary value and then treat it as though it were intrinsic. Fire making is not intrinsic to being human. We don't breathe fire from our mouths. We don't snap our fingers and create it. We don't close our eyes and "wish real, real hard" and...poof! Flames. Well...most of us don't.

Humans need fire, but we don't have it unless we make it, or scavenge it. Like a lot of things. We've never made fire that doesn't incorporate friction–and fundamentally this friction is on the molecular and even atomic levels, as is the factual case with

All Things. It also exists on the macro-level, in that *our* fire–human created fire–is merely a reconstitution of ancient fire. Actually, it's better said as "universal" fire, because truly stated, energy and matter are not created nor destroyed by us, merely modified. The fire we make is borrowed from the Maker of Life. As All Things Are, of course.

Do you think you can take over the Universe and improve it?
I do not believe it can be done.
The Universe is sacred.
You cannot improve it.
If you try to change it, you will ruin it.
If you try to hold it, you will lose it.

So sometimes things are ahead and sometimes they are behind;
Sometimes breathing is hard, sometimes it comes easily;
Sometimes there is strength and sometimes weakness;
Sometimes one is up and sometimes down.

Therefore the sage avoids extremes, excesses and complacency.

Lao Tsu, *Tao Te Ching*, 29

Scientists claim that there is no dark, no cold; rather the lack of light or heat. Yes, fire is many things. Fire is warmth instead of freezing death. Fire is light instead of deepest dark. Fire is both pain and healing. Fire is beautiful. Fire is terrifying. Fire is an embodiment of the Mystery that flows in all of life, and in part fire is what makes *us* what *we* are. Fire is ancient–as old as the Universe–and fire is brand new, all at the same time. Fire ends if it is not allowed to define itself, at least on some level; and fire responds to forces beyond our control. Fire is a primal tool that humans use to influence the eternal vastness of infinity. As well, is not fire a tool used by infinity to influence us?

In *praxis*, as a process, fire is an expression of a reaction that is volatile and degradational. Fire is duplicitous to human cognition, in that it may be the living expression of fission or fusion; each both destructive and constructive. For all practical purposes of *human dimensional fire*, it exists when materials reach a temperature wherein they spontaneously combust, beginning an energetic transfer on the molecular and atomic levels that degrades into subsequently more simple elements. Burning wood, for example, is undergoing a transfer of its cellulose and lignin—its mass, resulting in the release of energy (radiant heat/light), and the production of charcoal (elemental solids) and smoke (volatile elemental gasses). After the heat has dissipated (or possibly stored in some manner) and the gasses have distributed into ambiance, the only thing left is dead charcoal. Charcoal has many elements in and of itself which lend themselves to usefulness.

Why would wood—or any other material—spontaneously combust? Materials ignite because they reach their combustion temperature. This temperature is vastly different for variable materials. For our purposes in producing and using fire, we are keenly interested in the combustion "window" for vegetation. The planted world sources the vast majority of supplies for the human dimension of fire.

I would be terribly remiss if I didn't offer insights into the many aspects of the life of fire. Herein I am not intending to discuss exhaustively the nature of fire, rather the human dimension of it.

It is impossible to know when humans first made and controlled fire. As Carl Sagan said, "...there is no way to return to the past. All one can do is remember where one has been and carry that knowledge into the future." And another suitable Saganism: "Even distant stars will lose their lustre. Like dying embers unable to feed a brilliant flame they too will fall victim to ceaseless change in a restless Universe."

Fire is not human in origin. Apparently, fire spontaneously combusted at some seemingly infinite—but apparently finite!—"*moment*" in the "past" Universe, perhaps in the neighborhood of 15 to (?) billion years ago.

> In the beginning God created heaven and earth. Then, 'earth' was without form and a void was over the deep...Spirit hovered over water. And God said: 'Let there be Light,' and there was the Light. God liked the light and separated it from the darkness, making light the day and dark the night. Now there was evening and morning, and the first day.
>
> Genesis 1: 1-5

It was the illimitable life of Fire wherein Spirit Created Universe. "Earth"—matter—was *without form*. The deep—space—was a void. Spirit hovered over what was to be water—a product of fire—and was the tool of Life's Forging. Only after Light—fire—exploded into Being did the Maker separate water from "land"—matter. And although to make light, apparently it was necessary to create 'heaven and earth'—energy and matter—it took fire to bring the two together in such a way that All Life began. It does not matter to me the elusive debate regarding six days of Creation, with one day of rest. What matters to me is that expressing Creation in the form of 'days' is inherent to us, because *all we know as human beings is predicated upon lives lived in the day/night cycle.* Even contemporary scientists must use words that are inherently *relative* to the day/night cycle: the Universe (at current best guess) is approximately 15 billion *years* old. "Years?" *Whose years?* It is impossible for us to control the movement of the stars and planets, we do not manipulate the

celestial spheres, we are not Masters of the Universe...merely immature and impotent reactionaries to It. Argue this if you will, it is your breath to use as you see fit.

We do not know any exacts for when the Universe

Note the stylized serpent in this incredible Mayan architecture—"creator" represented in the horned, winged, anomalous serpent of myth. Serpents "breathing fire" have a globalized draconic familiarity.

came into being, and we are not aware of a tool available to measure the age of fire. Some of us *play* with words like "billions and billions of stars" or "billions of years ago," but honestly none of us is entirely capable of *imagining* what this might mean. We interact with our Place (Universe) through fire and its variable interrelationships. As we peer into the vastness of time and the void of space we discern pinpoints of light. In the past we surely

18

ascribed many whimsical explanations to the nature of stars. Our current whimsical explanation is that each star radiates light and heat energy from a point source of intense fusion combustion. This energy is a broad-band source, and infuses radially in *at least* three dimensions, but very likely in All Dimension–but we may never know what this means, truly. Also amazingly, many of the stars we view each night are not actually in existence anymore *except* in our perception of light...light exhausted indeterminately long ago. Ironically, and granted this is a deep twist that is challenging, even our *ability to perceive light and heat is inherent to our physical form which owes its very nature to the carbon atoms produced interminably long ago.* Our own sun–sol–is far too youthful to produce any significant volume of carbon (a heavier element, relative to the elements comprising the vast majority of matter), certainly not in the astounding quantities comprised in the earth's biosphere. Only ancient suns in dying reverberations inculcate energy into carbon–such a precious element, Universally–and yet humans so callously regard "the lump of coal." We would cease to function if our carbon relationship ended, period. We must consume it–in varying forms–so that our own internal combustion engine runs. Curiously, there are approximately the same number of neurons in the human brain as there are stars in our Milky Way Galaxy: an estimated 100 billion.

Nevertheless, fire–sourced–is enabled via the fusion of the simplest elements into ever more complex atomic or molecular form, which can subsequently be "diffused." Fusion is currently beyond human control, but fission and its processes are long known to humankind.

When something burns it enters a chain reaction transmogrifying matter. Energy and particles are released. Humans use both the light/heat energy and particulates of fire for many, many things. Our vast human culture is marked by this distinction in fire. No human culture is without fire. As human cultural revolution occurs, fire becomes more deeply imbedded in our collective psyches, as will be witnessed herein.

Rene Descartes (1596-1650) was in interesting man. In his life he expressed supreme confidence that the mind had the ability to discover God. One might assume that this opinion was predicated upon the concept that man—being created by God—was given the ability to percieve God. We might never know exactly where Descartes was coming from. It is true that this debate—the existence of God, and even the ability of Man to "know" Him—has torn the heart from humanity over and over. Sadly, even "Cartesian" thinking has led us down the primrose path to hell: mechanistic thought pretends to reduce the infinite to finite grasp.

Nevertheless, Descartes did strike upon a fascinating idea: *cogito, ergo sum.* I think, therefore I am. Descartes had found what to him constitutes irrefutable evidence of God in human consciousness—doubt proves the existence of the doubter. Doubt unveils the circumspect ego. Regardless, it is impossible to arrive at conceptual "imperfection" without conceptual "perfection." Hence—and like Anselm before him—Descartes realized that perfection not existing is a contradiction in terms. The experience of doubt, by nature, is implication of a Supreme—Perfect—Being.

To be frank, I *prefer* faith over intellect. This may be in contrast to what many might think of me. It would be easier, of course, if belief existed without choice, but this is not the case. Alas. We are made in the image of God. Evidently, God's Will is Free, too.

# Why Make Fire?

Light shines. Always has, all ways will.

**Why** did we even think to control fire in the first place? What led us to put such *intense* effort into not just producing fire, but also the development of rampant technological advances supported by fire?

My guess regarding why someone would invest such agonizing, embarrassing, frustrating but ultimately rewarding effort into the production of fire is this: curiosity. Moreso than the cat, it kills us too.

Also, though, curiosity has brought fantastic strides in comfort, medicine, entertainment, cuisine, convenience, and certainly in our overall joy and befuddlement as our awareness of Life is increased. We must not stigmatize technology as devilish —merely be intolerant of devilish applications of technology. Common sense leads us to a fair assessment of the value of fire as tool—without concomitant association with either demons or angels.

Karen Armstrong finished her fine work, A *History of God*, with these words:

> "Human beings cannot endure emptiness and des-
> olation; they will fill the vacuum by creating a new focus of
> meaning. The idols of fundamentalism are not good substi-
> tutes for God (*and never have been*); if we are to create a
> vibrant new faith for the twenty-first century, we should,
> perhaps, ponder the history of God for some lessons and
> warnings." (italics my addition)

Many would have us believe that controlling fire was necessitated by need. Likely we did not ascertain presciently the innate value of fire, and therefore did not approach the control of fire methodically, experimentally or with a particular goal in mind. The human animal doesn't have that kind of imagination, in general. What imagination we do have is clever in extrapolation upon current reality. Fire—having existed already in eternal infi-nite-ness for our ancestors, too!—was not "something to create."

The earliest commonly accepted evidence for the con-trolled use of fire by humans was found at a site known as Swartkrans, in South Africa. Dated around one million years ago, this site yielded carbonized bone fragments indicating exposure to temperatures associated with ranges known for campfires. The fragments were isolated in a sediment layer associated with the presence of *Homo* specimens (*habilis* or *rudolfensis*). So although the fire could have been used by *Austrolopithecines*, researchers have concluded that it was an early "human" instead. Oddly, the bone itself included antelope, zebra *and Australopithecus robustus!* Conclusive evidence for the control (and assumed production) of fire comes approximately 500,000 years later, in Asia. Hearths have been excavated at Zhoukoudian, in China. These early hearths are credited to *Homo erectus*. By 300,000 years ago evidence for the production and control of fire become much more commonplace, at least that is the interpretation of the paleontological record. Scientists will ceaselessly debate the *when* of the human gestalt of fire's mastery. Regardless, *mastery* of this element–as insinuated by the "at-will" production of it–may be relegated to insignificance in comparison to the fact of its ubiquitousness during the peopling of the earth.

Rather, it is highly likely that our ancestors *constantly* attempted to *keep the fire they already had going for as long as possible*. This fire might have lived for generations, and its Caretaker(s) highly esteemed among our predecessors. We know through anthropology that many, many humans place an inordinate value on their fire. Some people love fire to the point of danger, some walk on it, some juggle it, some swallow it, some play magic tricks with it, some write poems about it...and so on. Surely our cultural ancestry includes many such colorful elements, and with all certainty:  the person(s) assigned to taking care of the fire faces much responsibility in their social environment. This sense of "place" that fire maintains in our livelihoods permeates its way into surprising cultural nooks and crannies. Whenever there's a black-out–or even a brown-out!–we immediately demand service from our fire providers.

Those earliest "fire-tenders" were probably good-hearted pyromaniacs. As soon as new elements of fire became known–be it someone stumbling into the production of an ember when grinding two sticks together, never a "simple" task–or the subtle realization that boiled water used in cleaning a wound helps it heal...any new fire-thought was met with enthusiasm and trust. Fire is a friend to us, almost like a powerful leader that must be cajoled and placated. Nurturing a relationship with fire is a healthy thing.

> These are the regulations for the burnt offering: [it] is to remain on the altar all night...with constant fire...the priest—with clean clothes—removes the ashes to the side, leaving those clothes and attiring afresh...keeping the fire burning at all times, the priest removes the ashes to the prepared place...the fire must not go out...always the priests must keep it burning, each morning with new fat...the fire must be kept burning on the altar continuously; it must *not* go out.
>
> Leviticus 6: 8-13

And even though if you play with fire you will be burned, I suppose that once fire had been "controlled"—however intermittently—we experimented at once. Not only did we choose to harden wooden tools, or burn and scrape vessels, or crush charcoal to tattoo or paint...but we also played with the burning of *things*. Stone is changed when it is heated. Whether or not the "stone" is in the earth's core, or in the hearth, it will change. Siliceous material becomes glassy and brittle, finely flaking. Iron ions modulate their harmonics to align with the earth's precise electromagnetic moment while at the Curie Temperature and they will never

Accurate reproductions of Southeastern Indian ceramics, pottery by Michael Stuckey.

shift from it unless the Curie is attained again. This reality—phenomenally related to the migratory abilities of many birds, fishes and other animals—allows the modern archaeogeophysicist to accurately determine the location of burned clay (as in a prehistoric house floor) or quantities of ceramics (burned clay!). Fire treatments can have extremely unusual and useful applications.

If a person takes a brain-tanned animal skin and hangs it over a dampened fire the creosote oils encapsulating the gaseous particles we call smoke pervade the fibers in the hide and help protect them from water damage. As well, elements in formaldehyde and other gasses assist in breaking down the binding molecules in the proteins which could have otherwise caused the hide to stiffen. All of the hard work of softening a hide is preserved from ruin. What a great idea!

Fire. This tool is—perchance—the single greatest achievement of humankind. It stands to rank admirably with any mental gestalt the collective human consciousness has ever realized. And wonderfully, we didn't create it...merely learned to control it! The miracle we call fire is well viewed in light of the fact that energy focused and released as human beings manipulate heat, fuel and oxygen is an effort of will to "create" as well as "control." Fire out of control is a dangerous thing. Whenever a person exerts enough will to generate fire, that person is inherently responsible for the *entire* consequence of existence for the subsequence of its life.

I seriously doubt my ability—or interest—in listing every aspect of the human dimension of fire. Regardless, I *must* bring attention to its scope and breadth. Humor me.

Fire is light—cookfire, candle, torch, bulb, laser; you name it, there is the reality of light. Fire is protection—nothing likes to be burned, germs die in high heat, chemical reactions occur that can allow edibility. Fire is destruction—it will take down a tree to build a house or it can take down a house, it will herd animals and it can ensure the revitalization of the land. Fire releases active

constituents to be infused in tincture or incense—for communing with the physic or the spirit. Fire behaves both predictably and surprisingly, and has sponsored the same amongst ourselves. Fire powerfully conforms matter to our will, a partner in the creation of a vast array of generational tools and instruments—from cooking vessels to edges to hole-drilling and melting; from medicine to music and architecture to art, fire is there—indelibly.

And fire lives in our mind's eye, as well. There exists a relationship with fire that is multi-dimensional. It will not be possible to communicate what I mean, exactly, but I hope you understand the implications. I could give any number of examples, but within my desire for efficiency the following story is a marvel:

*Humans have remade the world in the image we desire.*

This is, in part, why we make the claim of being made in 'the image of God.' This is a dangerous claim. Certainly it is a phenomenal pronouncement: either it is narcissistic heretical crime against Life, or it is a fundamentally important mental gestalt—prophecy. It is a decidedly unique point of view, and, seemingly, only humans have entertained it.

It is *us* who not only made the claim—and please don't disclaim your *Homo sapiens* ancestry—but also very much us whom are exercising the apparent right to do so, and all of its associated influences and concomitant consequences. The current world system of human interrelation is funded entirely in a *praxis* reliant upon the *inherent human right to change the world to suit our wants.*

My mind merely *inherently* begs the question of 'do we dare assume so much?' First, we do not control the zenith of the known universe. Second, we do not even know where to look for such, or likely possess the skill, wisdom, acuity or comprehension to recognize it if it were discovered. Third, our 'assumptions' are killing us. This awareness cognizes a comparison to our antecedents–among other things–and their longevity and sense of mortality. Often we moderns compare ourselves to people long since bequeathed to time inaccessible to us, excepting the deafeningly incomplete view that the delightful pastime anthropology imparts. Nevertheless, a fulfilling (and as accurate as possible) perspective on what has come and gone before is in my opinion essential for a debative logic regarding Nature, God, Universe, Humanity and such concepts as Redemption.

It is very true that all of us are in some manner or way influenced as we fear death, question life, ponder meaning, explore options, react and *are*. And we *are* influenced in every way Infinite to us in every eternal moment that we attend to life. Does any know when life ends? Does any attest comprehension to the mystery of what we *call* life and death? Death appears as a disconnect from cognition of human souls recognized as immobilizing of matter. Regardless, interacting with cognizant entities during the tenure of this undetermined period (we do not have absolute prescience over life's duration) is enough to grasp that *there is spirit enfusing and enlivening all we are and know.* Who are we to explicate that which is not dictated nor determined by ourselves?

And so what if we remake the world in our image? We are made in the image of God, so doesn't that give us a right to pretend we have control—even when there is sufficient evidence to suggest otherwise?

Speaking of Infinite and Eternal—so what if a butterfly's

wings over Asia can produce a storm over Georgia? U.S.A. or post-U.S.S.R.? Forget the storm—that we will get over—but what about the rains that fell on (what would be known as) Egypt 'four-thousand-uh-eight hundred and-uh-forty-two(?) years' ago that allowed the desert to react and bloom in that rarest of human ways, ultimately begetting a civilization that lifted hundreds of thousands of tons of rock hundreds of feet into the air using mechanisms unexplained by a more "advanced" civilization that same much time later? So.

# ?

To each their own....
But guess what? *Fire* was the key which made it possible.

Yes, fire is a human determinant. Fire is power. Firepower thunders. Firepower parts seas. Firepower miraculously heals. Firepower wins wars. Firepower lends its wisdom to advance technology and efficiency. Firepower destroys. Firepower builds. Firepower moves mountains. Or makes them. "And God said: 'Let there be Light'." And the Universe flashed into Existence.

# Light
Light of Life
Shine!
Always enlightening me
Incessantly lightening my burdens
Light my way
To where I may light
And illuminate that Place brightly
Giving sight
Itself

29

Energize me not with
Your Comprehension -
Per se -
Rather, if nothing else
Then with the light likeness
That lit the Eternal Flame
Whose striking light
Deflects the dark
Radiating luminosity
An Infinity
Not gravitous
But lightly
Spirited

- like light spirits -

Mind altering
Not mind destroying

Yes!  Electrify me
With the magnetism of
Knowing
186,000
MPS!

Oh, Light of my Life
You shine on
Always having
All Ways Willing!

For all of time, throughout the universe, fire's vulcanism forges. Fire engages the natural world and manages the evolution of the myriad lifeforms which inhabit it, including us. Firepower, as harnessed to the human condition, is used to manage the land-scape in far, far more advanced manners than–apparently–any other earth-life-form.

Fire is the foundation of mechanistic technology, and is represented in all human lifeforms, and in seemingly all areas of human lifeways. And while to some the following quote will be enlightening (ahem), to others it might seem obvious...regardless, it captures my point well: "He [Alain Passard, chef of Arpege, in Paris] abhors the fire of undisciplined grilling, 'everything tasting of carbon.' For Passard, the essence of civilization is the taming of the flame." (Thomas McNamee, "How Great Paris Restaurants Do It," *in* Saveur, no.35, May/June 1999) Clothes, water purifica-tion, shelter construction, food production...music, art, architec-ture, medicine, travel, the light in your home, the "hot"dog so tastily consumed at the ballpark, boiling the ingredients to make beer, sterilyzing gauze...fire is ubiquitous. And yet fire is not inher-ent to human control. We *chose* to assume management of fire and now we are utterly *reliant* on it. Without *fire* our lifeway would *not be civilized*, and yet the decision to modify our behav-iour to base our livelihoods upon fire was our choice. It is *our* collective addiction–and one not to be broken. Is it from fire that humans must be redeemed? Or is it fire that illuminates our redemption?

Well! *Gawd* bless!

# Why Make Love?

**Why** do humans love to make love beside a fire? How is it that candlelight dinners lead to such....

Beloved–under the apple tree I roused you; there your mother concieved you, she who was labouring gave gave birth to you. Place me like a seal over your heart, a shield on your arm; for love is as strong as death; its jealous-ly unyielding as the grave. It burns like a blazing fire, a mighty flame. All the waters could not quench it, the River will not wash it away.

Song of Solomon 8: 5-7

## Eternal Lover

for so long I have waited
at the gates of Heaven's Heights
for the living rainbow filled with all colors
resplendent reflections and visions
rising from a new horizon
sparkling–tumbling–light cascading
The Waters Fall

shocking me, tingling me...
clear, pure and refreshing
a primeval offering of manhood's baptism

And is it not so with everyman?
*One* who moves you to transform from the sapling
into the oak, the willow, ironwood and cedar
then You say to me: "*what is it?*"
I must look as though I've something to say...
but no words with which to speak

"yes" is my breathless reply    agony
in needing                of wanting You
to know of the beauty in Your eyes
moreso when they look deeply into mine
agony of desiring            of wanting to lean into Your fragrance
Your essence    how it draws me near, home
more surely than the lure of water to sirens
a Nectar which flows with the rhthym of my Life

and You! so effortless You take me!
seemingly beyond my experience–therefore Yours -

so that knowledge is supplanted with wonder founded in a grateful heart

no hesitation, only endless questions propelling me
with forces and factors distant to my mind:
familiar and comforting in a timeless adventure
unexpected but cherished in entirety

"*do you have more you say?*"

yes.  curves                 homeland        mountains and valleys
strong with life—contours sculpted by the Master to hold, to give Life
to sustain
a breathtaking vista overwhelming my senses
and then Your voice!  silent or laughing
it thrums with pleasure
what a voice!  the thoughts which move You to speak
move me to remember          Your voice is a sound
which catches in my throat...
its dusky sweetness
a savored breath telling of You—of Your World
call me Yours

the sultry look that walks up and stares
the move that gets you up and makes you dance
the soft sound that coyly entices spontaneity

a gift immeasurable and unachievable
as only a gift can be

"*more,*" You say
More? oh!          a moment lost in eternity
why?                a moment lost in nevers

## Wild Fire

why not?          a moment pure and everlasting


it was there where Temperance fell to Life,
charmingly overcome
it was there where so sweetly did I know Your mood,
know Where You held Me
never before had I been held by You
            trap me in Your thoughts and laughter
                  cradle me in Your embrace
                        let me cradle You


Your design                  how can You Be
        molded    fashioned              shaped
to hold my heart
and yet Unknown to me?


but for my having known You,  am I forever lost in a maze of Your design?
am I designed for You?
Wound so tightly into destiny that the threads are spinning and moving in
my hand to write these words with Your face in my window, in the sky, in
swaying grass and sweet chorus of Night?


as a flame emanating from the *heartfire* of All Things:


what am i to You?

——

    It is supposed that in the initial aware-ing when Woman
picked from the Tree of knowledge of Good and Evil, she and Man
realized they were naked. That must have had a seductive side to
it, because sex sure sells today. So I guess that from Then on, we
have had this sultry element to human sexuality. I could go on for
hours, and likely you'd like it, but that would be unseemly.

37

Nevertheless, it is true that many a child has been concieved hearth-side....

# Prince Unrequited

The spark is become the flame
Threatening to consume reason
Nothing so far from the same
Which takes Everyman in season
Harvesting the fruits of unforeseen actions
Fruits to brew a bitter wine to drown
The sorrows, attempting to dowse
The Fire

Will she eludingly surround me forever
Like rushing waters or wind?
Oh, to breathe her air again...to be
Embraced and touching skin soft, fair
To have her radiance shine upon this
Poor face, to illuminate what I
Could be, would be, should She
Have me again

There is no forgiveness—no need
Only lost time, washed under the rocks
And tossed away callously by my greed
All good intentions, horrendously amok
I can feel the beast within, howling in strains
Kicking in my chest and other places
Poor creature. Crying out for his freedom
And begging mercilessly, piteously, to be loved and fed
And released from such hellish imprisonment

*Wild Fire*

Tick. Tick. Tick goes the clock
Counting my follies every hour and Second To None
Hearing the tock lock the door to my heart
Beckoning me to Never Forget...as if I could
Nor do I wish to, for that is
Her way The Nature of Love
My Love

Sweet pain. Bitter wine. Sophomoric words
To drive on this insanity play
Rescripted each day and fed to birds of carrion

—come what may -

I rest on an imagined bosom
My mind turgid
Like Her nipples
When Once Upon A Time
We were lovers
Mirthful
And fulfilled

——

In this ongoing effort to keep the home fires burning, be always mindful that enkindling success is met through focused provocative non-violent well-discliplined skill. Only then will you enjoin spontaneity. Failures occur. There are other times, so be prepared: *nunquam non paratus!*

# Communion

She is an entrancing sister to the sunset
Dusky skin aglow with shades of gold dust
Drifting softly into blood hued tones of umber
Sun touched neck set away from the
Even tan of her breasts
Her skin dancing to pleasing chills as I
Make love to the clouds

She flies next to me
Her curves reach and define my horizon
Beckoning me to come forth and explore
To experience and find my way
To rejoice in the wildness, the brazen need
To join with another

So deep that need
So filled with the rush of Life
And so desperately strapped
And gripped—whipped—by dogma

Or supposedly so

I think not, for all around and within
The urge is not diminished
Only punished and tarnished

Not for me. Never!
I refuse to walk when I can ride to the Hunt and
Challenge my own in the untamed reaches of the
Deepest Pleasures

## Wild Fire

Bring me the cup
And let me take nourishment from her vineyard
And feast mightily as I rest warmly
Beside Her fire. Lulled to sleep with
Her setting sun.

——

Just for general consumption, I thought I'd add a little something on what happens when a guy gets burned. Ahem. Just kidding. Actually, it is true that the shade—in multiple sense—of a fire is called the umbra, just as the dark planetary shadow-cone is. Apparently, when faced with fire, life casts a long shadow. Though not referencing literary exclusivity, peruse these words:

### UMBRA–UMBER–EMBER

Here we find a subtle impression—in the words of their various definitions—of the human affair with fire.

(poetry reprinted from *Blackbird Dreams*)

Yucca plant with dead stalk.

# Trade Tools

"*Homo sapiens* is the most intelligent, the most dangerous, and the most cooperative of all animals that have ever existed, but we must understand that we are not the final product of 3 billion years of evolution on Earth. Our species, like all others, is an evolutionary work in progress. Unlike other species, however, we have some ability to control our fate. We have the know-how to influence how the game is played out."

–Donald Johansen/Blake Edgar *in* <u>From Lucy to Language</u>

During my tenure as director to the Bennett History Museum and Funk Heritage Center at Reinhardt College one of my duties was to oversee the installation of the permanent exhibit *Tools of the Trades*. "Tools" is a pre-eminent American collection of antique hand tools circa 1590-1950. The tools represent mainly western culture bias, but also accurately portray the foundational array of tools used by humankind during the great technological revolution beyond hunting and gathering. This revolution has occurred within a cultural matrix which is species specific to *Homo sapiens*, and which is primarily defined by complex traits resulting in generational tools used to provide for five basic needs essential in human survival:  water, shelter, food, clothing and fire.

There are any number of reasons why a person should spend some time perusing a lovingly curated and complete set of hand tools, not the least of which is that we are immediately impressed by the inter-relatedness of *all* of the items on display. There are a surprising few foundational technologies incorporated by humans. Most tools are *composite tools* in that they are created not only using multiple natural resources (stone, bone, metal, fiber, glue, etc.) but manufactured within variable disciplines (drilling, cutting, grinding, burning, etc.).

Truly stated, each of us is a veritable "Jack of All Trades." Everyday, all of us must relate to the interconnections that flow in life; forces forging all that we have been, all that we are, and all that we ever will be. Tools are Us. It's not just that we like our "things," as some capitalists and anarchists so extremely argue. Frankly, it's because way too few of us grow pelts for warmth, use our sharp canines to blood the jugular of our prey, slice the visceral entrails of a kill with scrape-sharpened claws or run fast enough to catch a deer or outlast a puma. We are a physically *weak* animal. We are a technological miracle. Left alone, unclothed and with no tools—not even fire—how long would you survive if you awoke one fine morning in the middle of an arboreal wilderness?

Technology is a good thing. Evil application of technology is a bad thing.

I'm not intending to go into a treatise regarding human technology, but from practical experience I know that when people understand some basic elements of foundational technologies their lives are enhanced. Take computers and stone knives, for example. What fundamental element do they share? This really makes me chuckle.

When energy in the form of the blow of an antler billet (hammer) on the matrix of a silica-rich stone (like chert, or flint) is stored, the form of preservation is a sharp edge, a seeming happenstance to us. The truth belies our ignorance. Energy is transmitted and stored in variable degrees in different matter. Curiously, "storage" can be explained as easily as: one knows what is *there* in part by comprehending what is *not* there. As "energy" "races" along the matrix of silica, as in all things, some transmogrifies along the way! If it happens to "erupt" from the matrix, its manner of extradition happens to "preserve" a "memory" of that "moment:" a sharp edge.

Silica may also be used to "store" electrical energy (a physical manifestation—usually heat—of the relative flow of ionic energy between ever more complex or ever more simple states of being). We "piggyback" simple data—*bits*—in the form of "0" or "1" onto this..."process." Beneficially on the human scale of relativity, a tiny bit of silica can "store" a seemingly infinite number of "0" or "1" units, giving the appearance of vast storage space for information. The value of this technology is remarkably evident on the human scale. Silica—the fundamental element making stone knives and cell phones successful—also builds one lovely beach. But don't sunbathe too long, lest that big ball o' fire in the sky create an excessive number of free radicals in your own private ecosystem. Hot.

Thinking about foundational human technologies is fascinating. In my opinion, stone bashing, fire building, object throwing, hole drilling and the fiber arts provide for the fundaments of material culture. Perhaps there are others. To each their own. "Humans" apparently began stone bashing in the neighborhood of 2.5 million years ago in east Africa. Scientists credit *Homo habilis* or *rudolfensis* with these early "Oldowan" tools. We may never know if such stone tools predated or postdated wood, bone, horn and other types of raw materials in human industry, as they simply don't survive in the archaeological/geological record like stone. There will be more discourse on the nature of fire as a human foundational technology in the chapter on the bow-drill. But what *tools* are needed to produce and control fire?

*A sharp edge is critical.* How can a person procure a sharp enough edge—and how sharp is sharp enough? From whence comes the raw material? What expertise is required to manufacture the cutting equipment? How many sharp tools are needed?

Beyond a sharp blade, what tools are used to make fire? Depending on the method, a stout 18–24 inch length of cord is handy. Other materials? Tinder–and perhaps some type of coal extender–is essential. Wood–not so soft as to crumble, not so hard as to polish–to grind together yielding hot dust...these are also absolutes. Again, depending upon method applied, some hard object–a slice of sapling tree, a pecked and ground stone, a suitable bone–that will fit in the palm of your hand will be needed. This *pressure block* should have a bean-sized divot in the middle of one side, where a finger or thumb diameter *spindle* can rest. If using a pressure block, then a lubricant is very helpful: pine pitch, wild cherry sap, malleable kaolin (clay), rendered fat, nose grease, ear wax or toe jam, all will suffice to slick in a pinch.

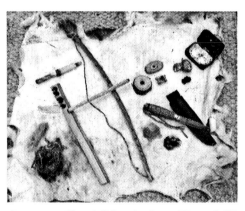

An array of "tools" for the basic "Bow-drill" kit: hearth and spindles, bow, cord, stone and metal knives, libricant, tindle, pressure blocks, and welcome mat.

Each method has particular requirements. Methods include the *hand-drill* and *fire-plow* (possibly the most ancient), *bow-* and *pump-drill* (related in form), *fire-saw* (material specific, primarily involving temporal and investiture constraints...see the chapter describing this technique for further information), *fire-piston* (an essential precursor to the infernal combustion engine), *fire-cord* and *iron pyrite/chert* (a primitive form of flint/steel).

The assortment of tools needed for such a variety of methods include a hearth board, spindle, corded bow or pump, lubricant, *welcome mat* (small flat platform to catch ember under hearth notch), pressure block, tinder and coal extender. An edge is essential to carve lengths, divots and notches.

Intuitively you are aware at this point that knowing how to create a sharp knife paleolithically was a survival ingredient for our ancestors. Indulge me in a brief outline of this process, regardless of the chain-saw, metal axe and high carbon steel pocketknife we all will use today to procure the woody materials for making fire.

Speaking redundantly, finding a local source for rock material containing high percentages of silica is important. Break lots of rocks. Find the ones that don't shatter or crumble. Look for strong sharp edges. The highest quality wild rock for flintknapping is a rarity. Don't be discouraged! Make do with less until you can advance yourself without jeopardizing the health of you and yours, and without perjuring your obligation to support healthy environments. One of the worst applications of technology occurs when *wants* become interchangeable with *needs*. These are not synonyms.

You *need* a sharp edge to work the raw materials (brush, wood, bark) into the proper tool configuration to successfully (and sustainably) produce fire. Sustainable means 'in continuance.' Resource and skill are the two relations of sustenance, made manifest in need.

You will find that a few different edges are very practical: a couple of thin-type edged tools (simple flakes or hafted stone knives), perhaps a thick-edged tool or two (hand axe or handled axe, either), and a bi-face with sharp serrations along one side—dulled on the other. The axe is to procure first generation material, the edged blades are to process the material into tool blanks–i.e. hearth, spindle, bow, cord. The serrated blade is ideal for grooving the notch into the edge of the hearth.

Now is an appropriate time to mention botany. Most of the raw materials for this fire endeavor are sourced from the botanical world. Beautifully, all plants contain silica, too, and some–like *equisetum*–have so much that they are like sandpaper! Nevertheless, the stone tools are not botanical–not anymore.

At this point you might be asking: "yes, please *do tell,* what woods will work for fire?" I have answered this question tens of thousands of times! Any would do. Any wood *could* do, but most would've won't. That's never my fault, but I'm still responsible, because I am aware of the "would-a, could-a, should-a beens."

Under heaven nothing is more soft and yielding than water.
Yet for attacking the solid and strong, nothing is better.
It has no equal.
The weak can overcome the strong;
The supple can overcome the stiff.
Under heaven everyone knows this,
Yet no one puts it into practice.
Therefore the sage says:

He who takes upon himself the humiliation of the people is fit to rule them.
He who takes upon himself the country's disasters deserves to be king of the universe.

The truth often sounds paradoxical.

Lao Tsu, *Tao Te Ching*, 78

Alright then! Let's move on.

# How Did You Die?

Did you tackle that trouble that came your way
With a resolute heart and cheerful?
Or hide your face from the light of day
With a craven soul and fearful?
Oh, a trouble's a ton, or a trouble's an ounce,
Or a trouble is what you make it.
And it isn't the fact that you're hurt that counts,
But only how did you take it?
You are beaten to earth? Well, well, what's that?
Come up with a smiling face.
It's nothing against you to fall down flat,
But to lie there—that's disgrace.
The harder you're thrown, why the higher you bounce;
Be proud of your blackened eye!
It isn't the fact that you're licked that counts;
It's how did you fight and why?
And though you be done to death, what then?
If you battled the best you could;
If you played your part in the world of men,
Why, the Critic will call it good.
Death comes with a crawl, or comes with a pounce,
And whether he's slow or spry,
It isn't the fact that you're dead that counts,
But only, how did you die?

—Edmund Vance Cook
(1866-1932)

# Troubles?

Fear makes the wolf bigger than he is.
German proverb

**Are** you troubled?

Guaranteed, you need to relax. Just sit back and take several *deep* breaths. Something that you should—need—to keep in mind is that *you are not in control.* But that which you do control will determine your approach to All Else. Although Western Thought attempts to generalize Hinduism and the teachings of the Buddha, it cannot be done. Nevertheless, the *anAtman* principle dictates that there is no existence independent from Existence. This whole big Universe is being directed by other than you, and this process of making fire? This process is virtually *entirely* controlled by other than you. You are merely supplicating yourself to the whim of All Else. Physics. Don't sweat it. Just remember that you and your insane—or should I say "inane?"—desire to force energy into transmogrifying matter from a semi-static state to a volatile reductionary reaction for whatever kicks you *want*; well (!) you might want to re-evaluate your priorities. Making fire by rubbing two sticks together is not at all practical in light of...in light of....hell, in light of your lightbulb. (boing) You don't *need* to know how to make fire like this...why are you even trying?

I'm with you. It's kind of infectious, isn't it? This whole little phenomenon we call *knowing*. There is a Sanskrit word, *avidya*, or ignorance—literally translated as "lack of light." It's a sneaky thing, curiosity. Gnosis: A Terrible Thing To Waste. So, you want to know:

$. What is this horrid squeek?
$. Did that spindle just flip into your eye?..sorry.
$. Is my finger bleeding?
$. Whu'd you saiy? Why *is* this notch important anyway?
$. What woods did you say worked? I've been using fat lighter like my granpa told me and I'm getting tons of smoke so I know I'm doing it right but I ain't gettin no umbro—or whatever you called it.
$. I never can tell when I should stop spinning the spindle...when do you know when you have an ember?
$. I kin make an ember right, but what do you use fer a tindle? (crikey)
$. How do you carve the notch?
$. Dangit! What woods did you say worked? I can't get fire for $ # ! +.
$. Is that *real* blood?
$. Uh, what do I do when I got fire in hand?

# DUH!

If I had a dollar for every time I've had someone ask me these—and other—questions, I'd be independently wealthy. If I'm writing a book on how to make fire by rubbing two sticks together, you may rest assured that I am not. But I can make fire with two sticks.

Actually, every fire ever made by humans has been with friction. You just can't escape physics.

Okay then. Back to basics.

I heard someone once say: "It's not that I'm good for nothing, it's that what I'm good at, they don't give a grade for." Likely. So, use some common sense here. You can force me to do math, but you'll *never* make me do math well. I just think differently. So be it. Oak doesn't make an ember very easily. If you burn cured oak in a fire already made, then oak makes coals beautifully. Two very different things, albeit related. The fiber and cell structure of oak is such that when ground under human-range pressure it produces either: coarse dust or sheen polish. If you don't grind it well, it polishes (and squeaks...whenever your *praxis* is cranky, change what you're doing, or with what you're doing it). *If* you manage (pro wrestler) to grind oak to dust, you'll find that most oak dust–from any oak tree–is too coarse to find easy ignition. Ahhhh. So the particle size of the ground dust is *important?* Of course. Ahem!

Now, for the exact same reasons that oak won't work all that well to produce an ember, it yields one fine coal. When vegetative material is less dense, it burns more thoroughly, leaving less volume of char, and having produced more volatile gasses. And vice versa: if a material is dense, it has more mass to convert to energy, so it will yield more energy, but less efficiently...less gas, more carbonized remains. There is a complex relationship in the combustion of matter that addresses the amount of radiant (light) energy released from the burning of a substance as well as the efficiency of matter/energy transfer as related to heat production.

Most *country* folks who've spent time around fire can tell you that pine burns hot and fast, leaving few coals, while oak or hickory burns slow and long, furnishing a cookhearth with long life and even temperatures. This subject has more than I care to invest here, but a good rule of thumb for making easy friction fire is this: don't use dense hardwoods, although some softer varieties work wonderfully...and are worth the experiment. Oh, yeah, the rule of thumb: if your thumbnail can dent the material, give it a go.

In the same process of thought: avoid material containing high rosin content. Resinous materials lend themselves to polishing—great for the "slick" end of the spindle!—horrible for the "business" end that might yield a glowing ember of infant fire. Any resinous material suffers heat entropy via evaporation, too.

If you have a problem with your spindle (hand, bow, pump methods) jumping out of its mated hearthplace, examine these possibilities: is your spindle perfectly straight? A crooked spindle wobbles—"wallering" out its mated hole into a sloppy oblong, or worse: rupture from the hearthwall...no good. Start over with a new hole and spindle. If your spindle is straight, look at the structure of its top—"slick"—end. Is the end strong and conformed to the receptacle in the pressure block, or crumbly and too big for the pressure block concavity? Also important in reducing spindle flippage—perhaps most important!—is *style*. Make sure that your body is in proper position for whatever method you are practicing. Note that the hand-drill has no pressure block—if your hand spindle keeps popping out—it is primarily an issue of strength, practice, skill. Keep one hand engaged with the hand spindle while the other hand fluidly rises to grip the spindle again at the top, finishing the hand transfer to top smoothly. Or you can learn and practice the *floating* technique (see *hand-drill* chapter).

If the method chosen mentions having a notch involved, then the notch is important. Don't go trying to avoid the inevitable or re-invent the wheel. Having said that, please also don't avoid experimenting just for the fun of it. Experimenting is different for a novice or an expert...keep that in mind! I've made many fires during the "mating" phase, where the materials were so good that no notch was needed. This is rare. The notch should follow a general "Rule of Thirds." The width of the notch should be about one third of the diameter of the  hole, it should fill up the center one third of the hole, and it should enter into the hole one third to one half of diameter of the hole. The notch needs to be as clean a cut or gouge as possible, and even in depth from the top to the bottom of the hearth. Hearths should be about finger width thick, and any length (within reason) will do. Enough to place your foot on (to hold it down) and not so much to be disruptive of the essential movement pattern per method.

Here again I will mention *style*. Every method has limiting pecularities. Most methods allow personal variability even *within* these parameters. Start with the options/suggestions within *Wild Fire*, but experiment at your leisure and pleasure.

# Principle Arts of Fire

"There is no try. There is only do, or do not."
—Yoda, Master Jedi Knight

**Fire** is an art, for sure. There is so much to know about fire! What a fabulous—virtually phenomenal if not for its ubiquitousness—creation. Fire is an awe-inspiring spirit. How must it have come into being? In what manner—or perhaps matter—and to what purpose does it exist? Are there knowable laws to whom are given governance of fire? These and other questions have bombarded my psyche for years. This is what I think.

Although no (one) way could ever provide comprehension of fire, humans certainly possess methods with which to explore it, as well as results from previous inquisitions. We have long been both infatuated and influenced by fire. Thousands of people before me have written of fire.

And yet, billions of humans—globally—live lives dependent upon fire without explaining 'what *fire* is.' What do *you* call fire? Flame? "Burning?" (...as if) "Combustion?" "Chemical process?" (whaa?) Fury? Love? Light? "let your love-light shine!"

Sure. It's All Good.

As mentioned earlier, "science" has given us many descriptions of fire. It matters not that science may never provide a comprehensive definition of fire–and its influence; what we *do* know is valuable, some say even invaluable. Fire involves combustion, a perpetually surviving praxis transmogrifying and/or transducing ions. It is the *infinite "Where"* that infernally confounds the human psyche. We are its product; its self-perpetuating sustainment. Fire is our fascination, our lover; our father and brother; the spawn and Lover of our Mother. It is our Myth; Our Mystery...no other animal we know for certain–soberly aside from Angels–possess It. Fire is our servant. If *Tools Are Us,* then *fire* is 'The *Tool.*'

It is a degradational procreative series of basic unrestrained chain reactions at certain temperatures resulting in the conversion of mass–or matter–from an initial state into subsequent states, releasing energy, volatile gasses and inert remains in the process. But of course it is so much more! The sun's fire may very well have characteristics unto itself–and likely others similar–but as it turns out, stars yield an extremely hostile research environment. A lot can be learned, however, from merely watching fire at a distance. Much more can be gleaned from the awareness of minutiae. Great pleasure may be attained by a dawning comprehension of the wholistic nature in fire. Quick and fascinating example: if one could 'stand' in the corona of Sol (our sun) they would be overwhelmed by two dichotomous points of fact–1. the corona can be up to millions of degrees, 2. regardless of this insane heat, they are freezing to death because that outrageous heat is not sufficient to fill up so much empty space. Weird, huh? Earth's atmosphere acts like a greenhouse, effectively overcoming this freezing void for surface dwelling inhabitants.

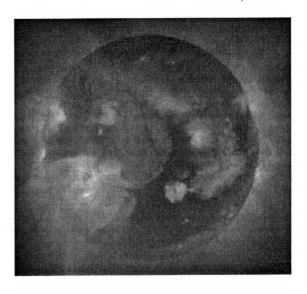

Four basic "things" are essential in fire: heat, oxygen, fuel, and chain reactions. In proper combination, these elements yield fire. If one is missing, fire is not inculcated. For humankind the re-creation and control of fire is an expression of *ego non-pareil*, in that on some level, fire must needs be controlled—or else it may unleash itself with devastating results! Fire exists on many levels outside of human control, and although we can *borrow* the entity we call fire for a time—in limited form—it is an inviolate rule of nature that all things pass from *this* state into *that* state. Change is the only constant. Therein the human dimension of fire dictates an egotistical element in the application of technology. For example, anyone who has ever made a fire from "scraps"—e.g. *rubbed* up an ember and blown it to flames—knows clearly that this element in the relationship between humans and fire is a challenging, sometimes debilitating one. The primary principle in the art of making fire is this: *make up your mind to do so.*

Success will be entirely reflective upon your ability to plan—and this book will lay a plan out for you—as well as your dedication to the willing of a fire to be reborn. It will not be easy, and due to human natural individuality each of us masters this skill at greatly differing rates! I have seen an elite military Ranger sweat over a fire-kit for an hour...the same kit with which I had previously demonstrated a thirty-second fire.

Amazingly, I have also witnessed an eleven year old girl–who had never laid one hand on a fire making kit–*put one together from kit blanks (notch cutting, tinder bundle collection, and bow assembly too) and* **hold fire in her hands** in about an hour! Unaided, excepting verbal instruction.

Consider the difference between the three would-be fire-tenders above mentioned: one is a 25 (or so) year old Ranger–male, U.S. military trained in the "survivalist arts"; one is a 30-something earthskills practitioner–well schooled to yield fire in most all attempts, usually in about 30 seconds; one is an eleven year old girl–mentally willing and able to *pay attention, replicate and mimic, apply flexibility and dedication.* She was *free* from the confining portion of ego in that her entire paradigm was focused on learning. Have you ever tried this? Apparently freedom from confinesof id/ego is a non-sequitur reflecting self-awareness. But regardless, that seems to be the essence of proper planning: admitting inadequacies to acquire 'perfection,' or as close as possible, right? What are *You* planning for?

The Ranger *never* succeeded in producing flames while in my presence. But if I know those military types, he has likely done it by now!

What have we determined to be the principle elements of fire making? One–*decide* to succeed. Two–*plan* to succeed. Three–*explore* each element of failure to *ameliorate* its influence.

Planning to succeed will be straightforward and you may feel free to jump ahead to the chapter on the bow-drill method.

However, if you are interested in this discussion keep on reading and learn more about *essential fire elementals*. I can only hope that my approach in describing them is entertaining and educational.

There are so many elements in fire.

Let's return to the four essentials for fire: heat, oxygen, fuel and basically unrestrained chain reactions. While keeping in mind that to humans there is a law that seems to govern the conservation of mass and energy, we humans are given a significant window of opportunity to "purchase" fire from the Universe. When we purchase something, we are making an investment of ourselves–be it commodity (including money), resource or labor–in order to obtain what we want or need. Remember also that wants and needs are not to be treated interchangeably, they are distinct elements of the human condition. I also find noteworthy the reality in defining *money*.

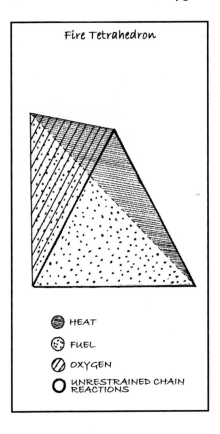

Fire Tetrahedron

● HEAT

● FUEL

◐ OXYGEN

○ UNRESTRAINED CHAIN REACTIONS

Today all of us use money in purchasing things. A more valuable view can reveal truths about money: it is a *symbol* used to define units of "value" associated with an assumed relationship between labor and resources. The supposed inherency of value is ascribed in (and from whence it draws vicissitudinal incipiency) many variables, including–among others–relative availability, perceived demand, perceived *Institutional* (read: **Government**) insurement, manipulated supply, egotistical expression of skill/knowledge (within the labor pool), and popular receptivity. There is *no* real value inherent *in* money, merely a tenuous and fluctuating commitment to the obligations alluded to in money's symbolism. Many who have amassed a "fortune" using this methodology become confused and depressed as the truth of their possession–or lack thereof–dawns upon them. Nevertheless, the incorporeal value symbolized in money can have *very* real impacts upon our physical world–primarily environmental, insofar as the perceived *power* is exerted without consideration that it might not be the *most powerful* option offered to Humanity as a Paradigm. Hey, it's worth thinking about!

Back to heat, oxygen and fuel. For fire to exist, each is not merely a want, but a need. Oxygen is usually in ready supply, although there is much to be learned regarding how much oxygen is required at each stage in the manifestation of a fire's life. For example, at the moment of conception–at and during combustion spontaneously incorporated upon the finite moment expressed in the fruition of a human will exerted over hyper-static organic materials–as the concept of an ember manifests physically, it is entirely possible to blow it out! Too much human wind in that moment might contain not only insufficient oxygen, but too much carbon dioxide–which kills combustion–and excessive moisture. Learning the balance of oxygen for the duration of fire is important.

Heat is indicative of the atomic condition of our universe. With the seemingly infinite inter-relationship of ionic energy embodied in mass–neutrons, electrons (and, yes, positrons), protons, quarks and all those quantum "parts"–there would be no heat in existence. As energy is released atomically, we feel heat. Even a free neutron won't stand alone, becoming a proton, electron and a neutrino with a half-life around 13 minutes. (!)

Light is an expression of this, too. The entire spectrum of light is a fantabulous thing...please look it up, so to speak. So, we can *absorb* sunlight heat, we can *borrow* second generation sunlight heat from the earth as it is released at "night"–which is a remarkably *rare* place–we can release and utilize multi-generation sunlight heat from carbonaceous beings–trees, grass, etc. We can also access ancient sunlight heat stored in fossil fuels. Earth's geologic forces also recycle sunlight heat in its core, generating heat/energy in many ways. Amazingly, the superheated nickel core of the spinning top Earth–which was formed from the ashes and gasses of stars–is a "super-conductor" that manifests a massive electro-magnetic force field which surrounds the planet. This also is worth much more thought than is allowed herein!  Heat is an expression of energy. To get heat, apply energy. Try to be efficient about it.

On the human scale for the manufacture of fire, we must have enough energy in our bodies (itself a tiny nuclear reactor generating electricity and radiancy, among other things!) to drive a *frictional* process to a relatively-known point of combustion. This point is usually around 800-825 degrees (F), according to Dick Baugh. There is a point of diminishing returns for the would be fire maker. The combustion temperature of some materials is unacceptable for our needs. Or, rather, some materials yield "fuel" or "heat" in proportions inconsistent with what is required by most human efforts to cause ignition.

Friction exists in a relationship between speed, pressure and surface tension. Generally speaking, friction produces ever greater heat at higher speeds associated with greater pressure and harder/rougher surfaces. Unfortunately, human strength and duration fall into a range where diminishing returns dramatically impact the attempt to manufacture fire.  It is better for us to modulate pressure, increase speed, and plan for a specific surface type. As surface is modified by speed and pressure, it is of great practical fire making value for the surface to yield *fine* dust.

Adding water into the interaction between speed, pressure and surface type is an unwanted variable. Although water *will be present* even in the "driest" kit, it is best in ever lessening amounts! Green wood and wet wood are of necessity distinct. Green wood can also be wet wood, but wet wood needs not be green. In fresh cut materials, the moisture enlivens the cell. In dead materiel moisture merely enfuses the fiber. "Wet," dead wood is still available for the production of fire. Only anecdotally have I heard of green wood yielding fire. I respect the possibility! Lesson: use dead, dry materials. Keep your kit out of the elements.

I have on *many* occasions encountered individuals who lie outright about their knowledge of making fire. Literally thousands of times I have received upon asking "who, here, knows how to make fire?" the answer: "I have." Usually this statement is made non-verbally in a timid hand-raising manner. When directly addressed as to what materials they successfully employed, and in what manner, more often than not–actually the vast majority of the time–the person responds with: "well, I haven't actually made fire, but I know how."

Okay now, there is clear implication in the question (hovering over a friction fire kit) and the environment (at some point during a discussion of ancient lifeways) that when I inquire as to "who here knows how to make fire?" I am referring to a successful flame inculcated through a method of primitive fire-by-friction. I expect such an answer as that which I so (sadly) often receive only from one who has the mentality of an immature child. Please pay attention here–or should I say, "please play fair"–there are three levels of gnosis: *learning* (hearing, seeing, reading, imagining), *doing* (hell, this means doing it!), *and sharing it.* When we choose to be generous with what we know, we invariably *learn* more, thereby increasing our mastery of a skill or lesson. Also keep in mind that our manner of pre-gnosis, or precognition, is imbedded forever in our perceptions. Our "way of knowing" –science–virtually dictates our perceptions, and therein our manner of expression. A clear example is found in the tiresome debate espoused by Creationists (so-called religious people) and Scientists (so-called rationalists). A majority of scientists are regularly not logical (and ironically this occasionally even yields the mental gestalt...gulp!), nor are creationists on the whole particularly religious (we *all* break the law)–regardless of their claims.

So neither he who plants nor he who waters is much of anything, but only God, who makes things grow. Both share a purpose, however, and each is rewarded by their labor. We are God's colleagues, God's harvest, God's temple. By the grace God gives you, lay a careful foundation on that which founds the Universe: Yeshua Hamashiach. Be careful of your foundation because it will be shown for what it is, the Day will bring it to light and the fire will test it for quality. If what you have built survives, you recieve rewards; if you lose it, you suffer its loss. And although you will be saved, your escape will burn you.

I Corinthians 3: 7-15

So, your gnosis is a very important thing! One of its best applications is determining your wants from your needs (best not be wanton). Also of credible validity is the benefit of ascertaining the impetus giving directive to your will. Mindfulness of circumstance is a good thing. It will usually lend itself to sensitivities which mitigate against displeasure and promote joy. This is valuable. It has inherent value, not like money!

# Hand-Drilling, and the People of One Fire

"[A]nd as the little water spider skittered from the water, exhausted, she rolled to her side and a burning coal tumbled from the web cup woven on her back. The Great Bear, Speaker of the Animal Council, called for the laughter to be silenced, as he realized that the tiny water strider had accomplished what all others had failed to.... She brought the fire...."
—Cherokee Elder story

**Perhaps** you are ready to lay hands on some primitive materials and twirl up a bonfire to cook hotdogs over...or perhaps sit around and bang drums...heat up *s'mores*? Maybe you are a serious student of human antiquity and yearn to learn the process of acquiring ancient skills in the task of seeking knowledge of your ancestors? Whatever.

In my opinion, the oldest techniques used by humans to *manufacture* fire would have been the *fire-plow* and *hand-drill*, respectively. The fire-plow is an incredibly basic *process*, and fraught with challenges. The very inefficient grinding technology of the plow is suggestive of great antiquity. Although it has subsequently been applied at great success in many ways, stroking is less efficient than spinning as a frictional energy generator. The fire-plow is not a technique that encourages a feeling of adequacy in fire-making. At least until you succeed! And discussed later along with the -plow is the fire-saw...obviously related. While bamboo works well as a -saw, you can certainly expend more effort and modify other appropriate materials.

The hand-drill is a far more approachable process, and will establish some parameters that are important in the success of later methods and technologies, namely the bow- and pump-drills. Now, pump-drills are very likely a much later addition, in that the clever fly-wheel contrivance elemental in the manufacture of the pump-drill (as well as the basic requirement of a cumbersomely heavy pump-drill contraption to succeed in generating an ember) precludes it as an earlier technique, being a cognition requiring preparatory fundamentals. Play with pump-drills after you have blistered up a few times over a hand-drill, and certainly after you are regularly pleased by the relative ease of fire production offered by the mechanical—but simplistic—bow-drill. The bow-drill is discussed in detail in the next chapter while explicating fire as a 'human foundational technology.' For now, let's address the construction and proper technique for hand-drilling a fire.

You'll need to locate the following materials: a sharp edge (pocketknife or stone), a spindle (vertically held vegetable stalk spun betwixt the hands, around 15"-30"long, perhaps one-half inch in diameter), a hearth- or fireboard (a plank-like board at least one inch wide, one-half an inch thick and approximately 8" long), a 'welcome mat' or coal platform (bark sliver, paper, leaf, etc.), a tinderbundle—or 'tindle' (shredded inner barks, grasses, needles, mosses, leaves, vegetable fluffs, etc.) and kindling sticks for an adequate fire-lay. All vegetable materials should be dead and dry, excepting "fat lighter"—or heart of pine (which usually is located in old, dead pine stumps) or pine-pitch, the sticky flammable sap. The tinder bundle should be finely shredded, and it is certainly possible to develop fire making skills to a high level...even producing a tindle is an opportunity for thorough-ness! The first time you fail to convert a hard-earned ember because of sloppy tinder you'll decide to reconsider the flippancy by which you might take my words! Harken!

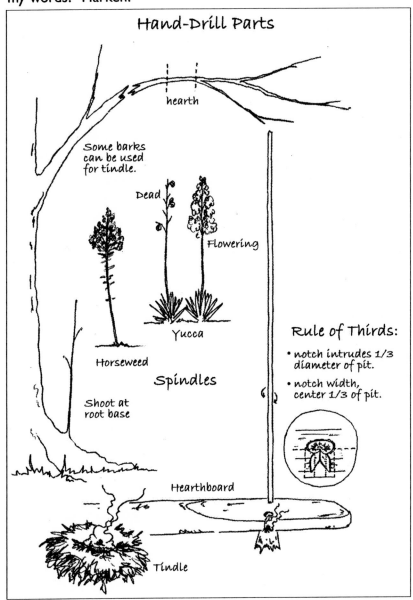

## Hand-Drill Parts

hearth

Some barks can be used for tindle.

Dead

Flowering

Yucca

Horseweed

Spindles

Shoot at root base

**Rule of Thirds:**

• notch intrudes 1/3 diameter of pit.

• notch width, center 1/3 of pit.

Hearthboard

Tindle

It is appropriate to experiment with a variety of materials in your area, though I would suggest a few specifics for the novice. For spindles, look for material that is already in the correct shape...per-

Snug tindle

haps mullein, cattail, horseweed, yucca, or shoots from the base of ash, willow, basswood and others. For hearths, utilize poplar, cedar, cottonwood, sycamore, willow, yucca, basswood, boxelder, and many indigenous *and* non-native species. Flatten *at least one side* of the hearthboard, but frankly it is so much easier if you find a suitable 'tree' that has a broken and splintered trunk or branch. The larger "splinters" are usually already "flattened" on both sides, and make great hearths. No wasted time, wood already dead and dry. Very parsimonious, especially since lots of these types of trees were broken by lightening or winds of thunderstorm. Appropriate!

Nevertheless, after collecting (and drying, if need be) your spindle, hearth, welcome mat, tindle, fat lighter and kindling sticks, arrange all of them within easy reach, and bring out your edge. It hardly matters what posture you choose to use—kneeling on one or two knees, or with your feet out front—you'll need to make the hearth fast to the ground. It must not wiggle. Carve a shallow divot in the hearth, emplaced so that when the spindle burns its seat the diameter will be completely encompassed. After taking time (don't rush or wear yourself out) to 'spin and seat' (burn) the spindle into the hearth (they should be closely mated, not wobbly or wallowed out), you'll need to incise or grind the notch into the side of the board.

# Hand-Drill
## (TANDEM!)

• Fire has always been a communal entity-
  make it so for your ember efforts!

• Two (or more) people can take turns.

• When you finish a pass, hold the spindle
  down in the hearth until the next person
  spins it loose.


BREATHE!

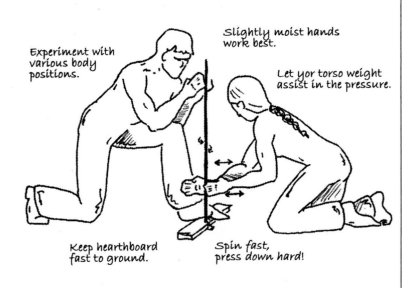

Experiment with
various body
positions.

Slightly moist hands
work best.

Let yor torso weight
assist in the pressure.

Keep hearthboard
fast to ground.

Spin fast,
press down hard!

It is possible to create an ember *without* having a notch in the hearth, but frankly it is such a worthwhile element, it should be used ubiquitously in any fire-kit utilizing a hearth-type board. The notch allows fine dust yielded via frictional grinding to collect in one space, insulating the incipient ember from cooler ambient temperatures, unwanted gusts and moisture. As well, the notch is physically positioned at the *edge* of the friction surface (where the spindle and hearth meet) allowing for the dust produced *at the height of temperature availability*–where velocity is greatest–to more synergistically transfer/modulate heat energy towards material combustion. Notch dimension is–if not crucial–certainly important. I have cognized that a "Rule of Thirds" generally applies safe and adequate parameters: considering the geometry of the carbonized circular hole (*not from the hearth edge, but the hole edge*), the notch should be one-third the width of the diameter of the hole, remove the center one-third of of the hole–opening through the hearth edge–and should reach one-third (to one-half) through the diameter of the hole; shaped like a pie slice. Use your sharp edge to score guidelines, preventing carelessness. The notch should be clean and even from top to bottom. The new ember will inculcate within the dust pile in the notch, tiny at first, but rapidly spreading through all available smouldering material. At first this material is the rest of the dust-pile, but you may add coal extenders–vegetative material from a variety of sources, including cattail and thistle fluff, certain types of fungus, fuzzy leaves like mullein, among others. A bit of coal extender is a great commonplace trick, worth arranging in every combustion attempt.

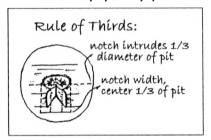

Rule of Thirds:

notch intrudes 1/3 diameter of pit

notch width, center 1/3 of pit

Once ember ignition is achieved, focus on safely transfering the glowing coal to your tinder. Nestle the coal deep within the bundle, but ensure that the tindle is tight and thick—albeit finely shredded—behind the coal. Gently blow to enliven the spreading ember, and solicitously embrace the centered coal with

all sides of the tinder nest. The coal should flaringly respond with every long, gentle, but brisk exhalation. Purse your lips and blow steadily directly into the nest, seeing the coal glowingly expand into the tindle. Turn and

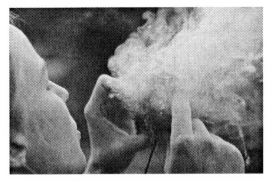

See the coal responding

manipulate the bundle *as little as is necessary*, but don't shy from the effort to keep the ember comfortably ensconced in the tinder's heart. Don't rush, but don't dither either. You'll get the feel for it in time.

All skills require diligent practice. Mastery is flippantly claimed, yet remains ephemeral and humbling. It's not *what* you know, but *how well you use* what you know. In the Koran (Qu'ran), al-Lah (God) sometimes recieves the divine name "An-Nur"—the Light. Now, An-Nur is *not* God, rather the praxis of divine enlightenment that is bestowed to the hearts of the willing. 'An-Nur' is the Light of Life. Nevertheless, it is sheer nonsense to attempt separation of divine enlightenment from Divinity Itself, as they cannot be independent. Divinity Is, as also we are offered divine enlightenment. Enlightenment is not *what* you know, but *what you do with what you know.*

Wild Fire

*Give up sainthood, renounce wisdom,*
*And it will be a hundred times better for everyone.*

*Give up kindness, renounce morality,*
*And men will rediscover filial piety and love.*

*Give up ingenuity, renounce profit,*
*And bandits and thieves will disappear.*

*These three are outward forms alone; they are not sufficient in themselves.*
*It is more important*
*To see simplicity,*
*To realize one's True Nature,*
*To cast off selfishness*
*And temper desire.*

Lao Tsu, *Tao Te Ching*, 19

You should expect to have some significant frustration as you learn and accomplish the skill of two-stick fires. It is an ancient human ceremony, and will promote fresh paradigms. I, for one, hope that you are amazed anew at your relationship to All Things.

Some specific trouble-shooting tips for the hand-drill method include special sensitivity to the downward pressure required in 1) keeping the spindle always mated to the hearth during exercise...every slip of the spindle from the hearth is a set-back in heat transfer; and 2) the actual pressure obligated by the particular vegetative components in your current set. Remember, be always concerned with the dimensions of your notch, but once cut you cannot replace. Be conservative. Has anyone ever noticed that those in western society (at least

77

**American) who claim to be conservatives often are among the most sinfully wasteful?**

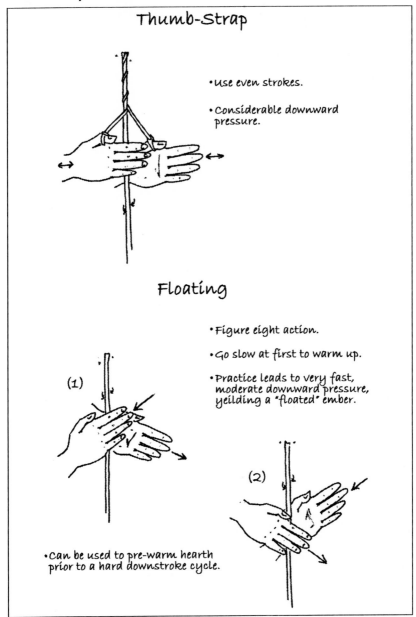

## Thumb-Strap

- Use even strokes.

- Considerable downward pressure.

## Floating

- Figure eight action.

- Go slow at first to warm up.

- Practice leads to very fast, moderate downward pressure, yeilding a "floated" ember.

(1)

(2)

- Can be used to pre-warm hearth prior to a hard downstroke cycle.

Hand-drill modifications include multi-person efforts or applying a 'thumb-strap' to the top of the spindle, effectively allowing downward pressure without the concomitant descent of your spinning hands. Usually an ember will not combust until the dust pile rises to the level of the bottom of the drilled hole. Many journeyman hand-drillers (me included) practice what is called the *floating* technique, wherein the practitioner skillfully, mindfully, works the hands in an alternating figure-eight motion at the top of the spindle. It is straightforward but challenging to slowly begin to twirl the spindle, never having your hands descend the spindle, and yet still coordinate speed, downward pressure and the prevention of anaerobic muscle condition to the successful birth of an ember. I believe it would be safe to say that—barring some ludicrous and jarring oversight in the training of a firemaker—if a person can twirl a fire with the hand-drill using the floating technique, that person has mastered the art of hand-drill fire making.

The more you practice, the more you will be able to make *more* fires with *less* materials. Your energy expenditure overall will become efficient as your skill improves. This is apparently true with most things in life, in that chaos and equilibrium relate in uncontrolled predictability. Perhaps Perfection exists at that ephemeral *interstice* of Their Meeting.

Anyway, most importantly:

**breathe.**

Breath is sacred. Your mindfulness of breathing will serve attempts to resurrect fire from the depths of time. If you fail to be mindful of your breathing, I assure you that you will suffer for it. This is a great place for some storytelling....

Some Muskogee speakers in the ancient American south-east expressed the sacredness in breath with an astonishingly prescient awareness of the nature of human 'wind.' *Hotali*—pronounced hoe-da-lee—is a Creek Indian word referring to human breath. Creek wisdom dictated that human breath was polluted—possibly in many ways; physically (odor), emotionally (vitriol), spiritually (malevolence)—and should never be used to enflame an ember for a ceremonial blaze (may the reader remember our contemporary scientific knowledge that toxins are expelled via our lungs—also a fragile front to our physical interaction with Life). Instead, a priest or acolyte would twirl a coal with a *blessed* kit and whirl the tinder in sacred movements using open air to fuel the ember into flames, then light the bonfire of the New Year Celebration!

Seeing as how lightning struck trees were sacred to almost all historical Amerindians (with associated archaeology correlates), there is parsimony in storm-chosen trees' *inherent* sacred-ness being availed for fire kit components...an expression of the multilayered relationship we have with our Universe. All humans share a basic cognition of spirit, and the spiritual dimension of fire is so vast in human culture that I will not belabor this story with them. I encourage you to imagine freely while sharing non-violently...I love to be exposed to altering perspectives, but I never like to be told the way to be. Leave that up to me, and I'll do the same for you. Or at least politely try!

Anyway, during the formal Busk—Green Corn—gathering each summer, the Muskogean Peoples would leave their homes in entire darkness. Void of fire, houses and entire villages were cold and desolate. Old, used pottery (and likely other fire-related products and goods) were ceremonially destroyed and replaced with new (therefore pure) items. Once the population congregated at the main township—like Cahokia or Etowah, Moundville,

80

or any of a thousand pre-Columbian paleolithic chiefdoms and city-states–the last few fires were extinguished. As the People waited in utter darkness–hungry from fasting, perhaps cold from a rain, excited to begin the new year afresh–a priest enkindled the sacred heart(h)fire of his flock–a tiny piece of the Sun, from which All Life emanates. Sacrificing the blessed kit to the youthful blaze, the priest inaugurated the new year.

When all returned to their homes tired from hours and hours of dancing, facing the rising sun, breaking their fast and carrying a live coal from the Sacred Fire, life returns to the mundane as coals become fires, who cook, clean, cauterize, sterilyze, smoke, sear, heat, enlighten, snap, crackle and pop! their ways into each facet of life. For the entire year, whenever one of these fire-children passes into cool sleep, the hearth is re-kindled with one of its true siblings, borrowed from a neighbor who borrowed from a neighbor, and so on, tracing unbroken ancestry to the Heart of the People.

One human will working with one kit to make one fire for one People for one year. One chance enabled by one Spirit. All things are related in *at least* One Way. What a beautiful thing.

He who makes his own fire warms himself  twice.

# Mechanics
# and the
# Bow-Drill

"Knowing our place in nature enriches us beyond comprehension. Nature is familiar, it is in our genes. It is re-awakened when we sit around a campfire and exchange stories, just as our ancestors did for hundreds of thousands of years when we were hunter-gatherers, living in tune with the natural world."
 –Donald Johansen/Blake Edgar *in* From Lucy to Language

**Though** there will be some who dispute it, and regardless of the given antiquity of drilling–along with bashing–it seems to me that a more suitable candidate for 'most ancient' would be the persistent, aggressive (fire is anything but passive) nature of *grinding* (i.e. the fire-plow) as yielding the tale-tell smoke absolutely imperative to lure the human consciousness to such devilish details, no? I really won't get all heated up if you don't agree, for whatever your reasons. To each their own. We likely will never know for certain which method was first cognized as a reputable technique in the manufacture of fire. For all my opinions, I will be the first to acknowledge that I don't know everything there is to know about fire. I do admit being a compassionate pyromaniac.

I would repeat that there are no 'non-fire' people. It is likely that the controlled regeneration and subsequent technological processual revolution unleashed through humankind's use of fire serves as the primal gestalt giving testimony to the unique

nature of our specie. Symbolizing our greatest tragedies and tri-
umphs, a constant companion in all of our conquests–be they
intellectual, spiritual or physical–the literal symbol of our inventiveness...fire represents the human spirit. Fire represents Spirit,
period, and always has. The *power* of fire has forged the destiny
of humanity. Upon its foundation, we built our temple.

Ever noticed that God's Voice exists in fire, and the devil's
damnation is all consuming? Does it strike you as curious that a
husband's passionate love is an Eternal Flame that burns out of
control, and enmity between states is referred to as a 'hotspot?'
How could it not have fueled curiosity in our kind when 'bad'
water–not good to drink!–is made potable when boiled? Such is
fire. Pandora's Box. A New Paradigm. The miracle-worker! Our
craven souls narcissistically seduced to a servant who is our
Master.

> The axe is already at the roots of the tree! Any
> tree that doesn't produce well will be cut and burned! I bap-
> tize with water, for repentance, but One will come after me
> far more powerful than I, whose sandals I am not fit to carry.
> He baptizes with Holy Spirit fire! Whinnowing fork in hand
> he will thresh the floor, gathering wheat and burning the
> chaff in unquenchable fire!
>
> Matthew 3: 10-12

Any way you look at it, human fire power has affected
Earth's biosphere with greater audaciousness than apparently any
action by another specie, excepting perhaps the bacterial release
of gasses? We are certainly responsible for the fire we use.
Everyone is. That is why there are so many disillusioned pyromaniacs steaming in jail.

From the Fire Revolution humans have explored a dynamic and intriguing melange of technologies.

*Prometheus* means *prescience*, precognition–foresight–in Greek. Intriguing.

On the one hand, fire was merely enveigled from the holy forge of creativity...on the other hand, borrowing fire from the Divine Hearth stole the power of creativity. Sounds like half full, half empty to me. Either way, fire incurred a state of being cursed forever with the doubt of not knowing how things would turn out. Literally, we invested (Vesta is the divine 'keeper of heaven's flame') in Pandora's "Box." (you sexy thang!) Woman–maiden–vestal virgin Pandora is the *final* repercussion for the theft: a blessing and a curse to man, integral to life. (In case you aren't all that familiar with ancient Greek myth, when "first man"–the demi-god Prometheus–"stole" fire from [either] Hephaestus' forge / Zeus' hearth, ushering in the age of civilization [hence, 'first *man*'] his initial punishment was to be nastily chained to a moutainous rock whereby vultures ate his liver each day, rejuvenated each night to suffer again the next day.... He was relieved from this hell by Zeus–who desired information about a certain sea nymph–and of course the nymph herself. In capricious competition with Poseidon, Zeus exchanged [for the information] one punishment for another [hey! no mortal ever really gets away with negotiating with Divinity!])

> Prometheus is the Jesus of the old mythology. He is
> the friend of man; stands between the unjust "justice" of the
> Eternal Father and the race of mortals, and readily suffers all
> things on their account. But where it departs from the
> Calvinistic Christianity, and exhibits him as the defier of Jove,
> it represents a state of mind which readily appears wherever

the doctrine of Theism is taught in a crude, objective form, and which seems the self-defence of man against this untruth, namely, a discontent with the believed fact that a God exists, and a feeling that the obligation of reverence is onerous. It would steal, if it could, the fire of the Creator, and live apart from him, and independent of him."

–Ralph Waldo Emerson, *Essays* (1803-1882)

I don't know about fires' being all *that*, but I'd allow that it does seem to me that fire is an intermediary between human mortality and the Unknown Eternity–Ultimate Reality. So, yeah, I can see fire as Judge and Redeemer. And it does seem clear–coincidentally (do those exist?)–that the human use of fire is the prime example of the fruit we picked from the "Tree of Knowledge of Good and Evil." And we sure consumed it heartily. Now if God is the Eternal Infinite, wouldn't it fit that Prescience would ensure the very *fruit* of Its Existence which gave us knowledge of good and evil–our judgement–also Redeems? It would be the *one thing* that Seduces us all, sooner or later...and the One Thing that *asserts the undeniability of Our Existence.*

"Fire is the ultra-living element. It is intimate and it is universal. It lives in our heart. It lives in the sky. It rises from the depths of the substance and hides there, latent and pent-up, like hate and vengeance. Among all phenomena, it is really the only one to which there can be so definitely attributed the opposing values of good and evil. It shines in paradise. It burns in hell."

–Gaston Bachelard, *Psychoanalysis of Fire*

Zeus' supremacy over the Greek gods was symbolized by lightning, or the power to cause spontaneous ignition. We respect the chaos embodied in fire with words like *holocaust*, [sic] entirely burnt (Greek). Human beings have recognized since time immemorial that fire is the natural rejuvenator of life, empowered first with destruction, and then ushering dynamic resurrection. The phoenix is both entity and process. Fire is *Fyr* (Anglo-Saxon)–*Pyr* (Greek)–purus (pronounced: *p(h)oeuris;* itself an ono-matopoeia when said correctly) [sic] illimitable dynamism in Pure Life (Latin). The 'fires from heaven'–lightning–are the instruments of Divinity...unpredictable, violent, capricious, Awe-Full. Lightning's suspect culpability in the foment of EarthLife itself inspired by cloudform whose existence is owed to both its mat-ter and its inevitability as the oceans are roiled by the heat and the winds engenerated by Sol's gravitous greedfeast.

Curious as to what all this has to do with bow-drill fire kits? Well, not much...and just about everything. You see, we humans have been battling it out for thousands and thousands of years trying to assuage our collective guilt by promoting our righteousness as the true children of God. It is ironic, granted, but it is true. We claim righteousness and insight into the nature of God (or the lack of Its' Existence, based on a species-specific [ack!] dim set of criteria), all the while struggling to accept our teeming imperfections. How could a perfect God create imper-fect things? Perhaps there is no God? Perhaps we simply aren't obligated to seek God and offer reverence? Perhaps after the creation occurred, something happened to us–or maybe we made some decisions that could have been better? Did we bring imperfection upon ourselves, or were we made that way? Hey, isn't it 'easier' to just let it all be chance? Random evolution of Mindlessness. (tsk, tsk)

This Universe—for all its grandeur—seems so horribly unjust! It is apparent that we need an intercessor...something or some One who reconciles us to the past, present and future. We need redemption. Fire is—somehow—an embodiment of the human soul, a material reflection of that part of us which is created in the image of our Maker. Fire sacrificially gives itself even as it exhausts itself. Fire imbues the human dimension solely because of our creativity—a manner of thinking and doing. Human creativity—such a limitless inferno—is also exhausting, inevitably requiring refueling. Regardless, be it enkindled or scavenged, it is to fire that human culture is engaged.

So, what are the fundamentals of human culture? I hate to be vague, but everyone pretty much has their own ideas on what it means to be human. For me, in this ongoing discussion on the human dimension of fire, it seems opportune to demonstrate firstly how human creativity links ideas and resources in clever ways, often diminishing human energy expenditure while providing ever 'greater' yields, be what they may. The bowing-a-drill two stick fire method is a simple but great example.

What I'll do first is outline what the bow-drill is—praxis and structure—and then expound a bit on mechanics and the influence of both fire and fire-related technologies. Herein lie fundamentals of human culture.

> "When you have crossed the stream that bounds two continents press on, over the surge of the sea towards the east where the sun stalks in flame..."
> (Prometheus speaking to Io) Aeschylus, *Prometheus Bound*

Now although you'll see that learning to use a bow-drill is—in its highest personal effecaciousness—a uniquely solitary accomplishment, it is *not* necessary to (initially) master the indi-

# Bow-Drill Parts

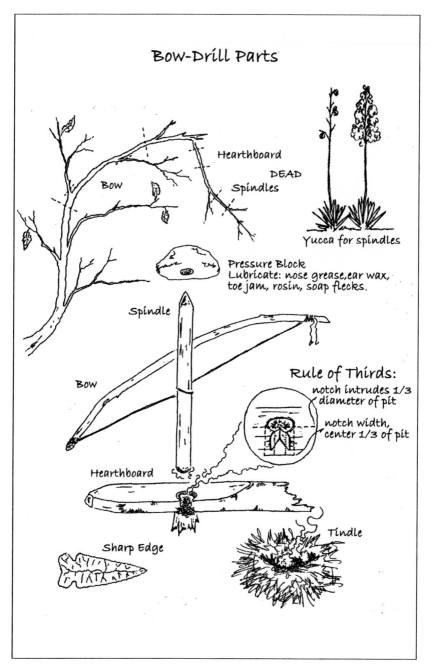

Bow

Hearthboard

DEAD
Spindles

Yucca for spindles

Pressure Block
Lubricate: nose grease, ear wax,
toe jam, rosin, soap flecks.

Spindle

Bow

Hearthboard

**Rule of Thirds:**
notch intrudes 1/3
diameter of pit

notch width,
center 1/3 of pit

Sharp Edge

Tindle

vidual production of fire. Humans don't live in a vacuum...we are not islands. People who take hermitage indefinitely are inevitably percieved as *not normal*–regardless of other perspectives of them. Let's introduce a tandem method of '*bowing-a-drill*' wherein you will develop subtle comprehension of the many dynamics of mechanism.

Contrive some new items for a bow-drill kit. Along with the familiar sharp edge, a hearth, the welcome mat, tindle and kindling, you'll need a new spindle (this one can be a bit thicker than the hand-drill, up to an inch diameter or so, but shorter...only about 6"-10" long). Also locate a *pressure block*. This can be most anything, the easiest is a section of hardwood. Or try a pecked stone or bone/antler–it needs to fit comfortably in the palm of your hand, and

Bow-drill assembly on hide

you'll need a smoothed socket carved into the center of one side. Lubricate the socket of the pressure block with nose grease, ear wax, toe jam, soap flecks, pine pitch or cherry sap...or whatever.

The *bow* in a bow-drill *occurs* twice: anytime you torque material (spindle being spun) too-and-fro, it will be *bowed* (regardless of if we percieve it or not), or broken Also, of course, the 'stick' used to handle a taught thong in making fire is a non-flexing object, so get the bow-and-arrow idea out of mind. A large rib-bone works wonderfully, but a dried bent branch is just fine. The cord for the bow needs to be first of all strong, secondly flexible. For this reason hand twisted rawhide makes a great narrow cord for the bow-drill, but the best is braintan! If raw hide—much less braintan—isn't

Sap on cherry tree

Cording fiber; each strand is twisted alone, but counter-locked together

available, experiment with cordage of Dogbane (Indian Hemp—*Apocynum spp.*), yucca(s) (Spanish Bayonet, Devilgrass—*Yucca spp.*), milkweed (*Asclepius spp.*), or any other strong-ish fiber. Or go for your shoelace, electric cord or nylon string.

The tandem "drill-string" is: prepare your hearth for spindle emplacement (see previous chapter); one person holds the hearth with their foot, kneels on the other knee, and holds the pressure block rigidly on the spindle. The other person kneels on both knees in front of the contraption, wrapping the spindle *once* with a ~20 inch string (*lightly* rosined/waxed/oiled is good).

Two or three youth can "string-a-drill"

Personage 'Holder' presses firmly down while Personage 'Spinner' begins swiping the string back and forth. 'Holder' tentatively lessens pressure until spindle spins, then holds steady. 'Spinner' coaches 'Holder' in increasing/ decreasing pressure while being attentive to: spindle bi-rotationality, verticality, mating surface integrity, speed, (did you carve your notch?), dust accumulation, color of smoke, ignition. Inculcate your ember on a welcome mat, to ease transfer to a tindle.

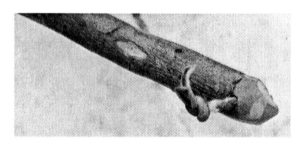

Use quick adjusts for your "knot" on the bow

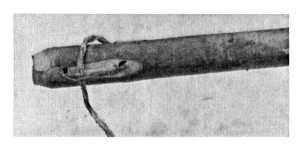

If you are at the stage of trying a bow-drilling fire *alone*, tie the cord somewhat loosely to your 'stick'-bow–loose enough to entwine your chosen spindle at least *once*. It helps to learn to enloop the spindle so that the slick end finishes *up*, with the spindle body *to the outside of the string*.

Configure your body in these stages: arrange your materials in front of you, kneel on your dominant side (though later you should practice ambidexterity), place your non-dominant foot on the board–barefoot is good, hearth under arch, one finger width from hole edge, lean up and off your rear, hovering over the board. Pick up the bow with your dom-

Organize your work space

inant hand, at one end. Use your other hand to pick up the spindle and twist it into the bowstring. There are various techniques

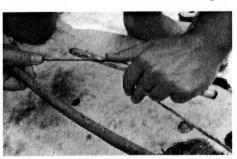

Twisting spindle in bowstring; remember to finish with "slick" end up

to do this, very personal. Create your own, but be aware that once you choose a "slick" and "business" end for your spindle you should plan never to switch. Therein I find it a better configuration to have the spindle twisted in such a way that it finishes vertical, with slick end up and spindle body on the *outside* of the string. Whatever, just pay attention to which spindle end is which. Seat the embowed spindle into a divot in the hearth and use your (dominant) fingers to stabilize it while you reach (non-dominant hand) and position the pressure block on top of the spindle. Let your non-dominant arm rest outside your upright knee (non-dominant leg, holding board), with your hand gently but firmly holding the block, wrist bent and held snug against your shin. Begin with short strokes, immediately progressing to *long, even*, smooth strokes...using the entire length of cord.

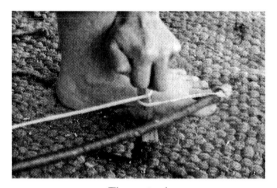

The action!

No need to go full blast at first, as you have to do two things prior to achieving an ember: seat the spindle by burning it until it is flat in the hearth...and carve appropriate notch. Then resume drilling to drive the moisture from the materials, raise the temperature and create a notch-pile of dust to the level of the bottom of the working hole. Once the dust pile is evident and smoke has begun, methodically increase your speed and downward pressure in a roughly 2:1 ratio, speed should be twice as dramatic as pressure. Smoke should billow forth from the mating area.

Carving notch

95

# Bow-Drill

• Bow-drill assembly wants to fly apart... like a helicopter... so try and keep all parts strictly under control.

BREATHE!

Keep torso centered over spindle and hole.

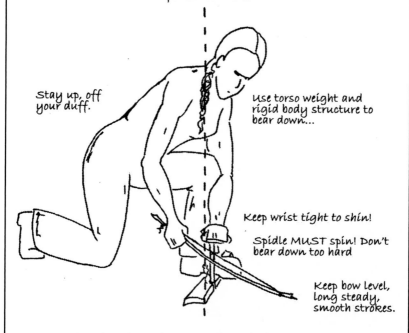

Stay up, off your duff.

Use torso weight and rigid body structure to bear down...

Keep wrist tight to shin!

Spidle MUST spin! Don't bear down too hard

Keep bow level, long steady, smooth strokes.

Foot on hearthboard: "finger width" from working hole; board under arch; hold hearth fast to ground; Try it shoeless, it's easier!

A tip to know when you can slow down and stop, having achieved combustion: watch the smoke in two ways. One, where is the smoke appearing? All around the spindle, or primarily over the dust pile? Two, what is the color of smoke? In the beginning it will be white and whispy, coalescing to a more bluish hue as the temperature approaches chain reaction combustion release. A live ember gives off a dirty, yellowish, thick smoke.

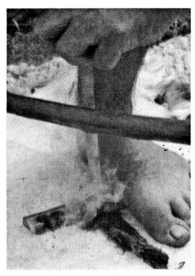

Watch for the smoke to change.

Don't let the spindle wobble, keep it vertical. Hold your pressure block hand *snug* against your shin. Stay up and off of your rear. Long, steady strokes. Check dust to be sure it is fine, not coarse or granular.

### Breathe!

When you incite a spark, tindle it. Oh, and by the way: you don't have to waste an entire bundle to get a nice campfire.

Mr. Redford as *Jeremiah Johnson* committed a woodsman's *faux pas* when he plunged his lit tindle underneath his fire-lay. A true practicing primitive is invariably a conservative liberal at heart. Learn to use a sliver of fatlighter as your *welcome mat* and then leave it inserted in the tindle while you coax the flame. By the time it flares up, the pitch is liquified and ignites too, allowing you to transfer the flame to your fire-lay...while extenguishing your precious tindle! Even earthskills "master woodsmen" are sometimes surprised by the initiatives of their initiates....

Smoke rises; remember to hold tindle up

Use fatlighter "match' to transfer flame to fire lay

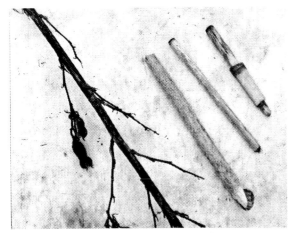

Assortment of spindles; Yucca stalk, yucca spindle, horseweed spindle, and bone spindle extender with yucca plug.

Assortment of tinder and kindling.

Cedar bark, "nest" of cedar bark with cattail fluff, and cattail fluff.

Yucca plant with dead stalk.

Snug tindle

Horseweed

Polypore fungus and tinder

Body Allignment; top view

Gather fuel of all sizes.

Please keep in mind that there is a lot more going on in the process of bow-drilling a fire, say as compared to the relative simplicity of the hand-drill.  Now even though the quantum physics dictating the transmutation of mass and energy inculcating fire are operating in concordance with Universal Reality, the bow-drill is *fundamentally different* than the hand-drill technology. In the bow-drill we see the human willingness to expend more effort *up front* to save energy *later on,* especially a security in greater success percentages. The manufacture of a bow-drill set involves more time, knowledge, insight, planning, awareness of resources and a subtle yet imperative intuition regarding risk and reward. Necessity needs *not* be the 'mother' of invention, as so many have claimed, in that while the human *want* for fire indeed necessitated its flagrant control; *exploration* of the vagaries of its production, mechanics and relative technologies are not predicated upon our basic need for it. It was *not* necessary to control fire for the survival of the animal we were, or that animal would not have been. It is our addiction to fire that procreated our need for it, and now we cannot survive without it. Our use of fire always has been and always will be a choice.

So we see that awareness sparked by the control of fire is a harbinger of further mental gestalt (thus an idea "sparks" in our

minds), inter-weaving the physical, emotional, intellectual and spiritual. We also see the deepest depravity of the human condition: celebration of self-imposed enslavement. Whereas fire in and of itself contains no good or evil; fire as an embodiment of our *almost* justified hubris and ultimate willfulness towards Infinity illu-

minates our sin, our *misdemeanor*.

It is no wonder that once we collectively agreed that having sampled the forbidden fruit of knowledge of good and evil—

insolent *self*-destination, with fire as our primal tool—we began a race against ourselves. Without the burden of God's judgement (though many—nay, *most*—of us continue to deliberate upon God),

1000 Columns; Mayan ruins at Chichen Itza

we competed against the two "gods" vying for our adoration: Power and Nature. Fighting chaos—of supply and demand—we made a battlefield of both humanity and the natural world. It is still self-evident that this choice is inherently destructive. Ironically, throughout it all, *fire* preserves its innocence. *The enemy is known...the enemy is us.*

Ahh. But along with the wildfires, fire hardened spears, heat treated arrow points, steam bent bows, slash and burn agriculture, smelted and tempered swords, flashing gunpowder, over

population, the industrial pollution revolution, holocausts and torture...there are the infinite blessings, too. Herein fire again is the voice of Ultimate Reality: energy and matter are not created or destroyed. What was in the beginning will always be. As

are we not Unmade. Our foibles and misdemeanors are not outside the power of the Universe. Blessings come, like the Phoenix, resurrected from the ashes of our misunderstandings. Beyond our control, this is testimony of Spirit Immortal. To wit: from weakling with no admirable claws, predatory fangs, warm winter pelt, flashing speed or thundering strength...a tiny chance encounter with a thought transformed a feeble population into *the* global powerhouse of innovation.

As witnessed, culturing fire–from coaxing an ember to smoking braintanned deerhide to lighting an altar candle–is always best accomplished with companionship.  Herein exists the beating heart of culture: fellowship. Family. Community. Commonality.

See, we humans *share* so much more than we differ; and we also share this commonality:  domestication of fire.

With fire our ancestors enabled a food base proportionately greater than they had previous.  Our distant ancestors were technically omnivores–however herbivorous most meals may have been–as we are, yet fire provided a manner in which the toxins in previously inedible vegetable foods were broken down, or their effects ameliorated. Although maintaining digestive designs to consume a primarily herbiv-

Smokin' jerky

orous diet, we suddenly could modify flesh protein to make it easier to digest even *in* the current intestinal system...and which concomitantly assisted in the preservation of extra meat.  A greater food base, in variety and quantity, generated more avail-

104

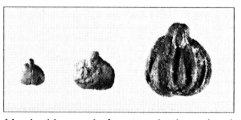

Marsh elder seeds, fortuitously charred and preserved archeologically.

able energy to be synergized by the body in any way encouraging sustainability—especially in the long term: thousands of generations. The energy made ever more available by the efficiency inherent in fire technology has basically been expended in the operations of our brains. Inside our brain, which is intrinsically connected to all of our other parts who interact with Known Reality, we have cognized a Mind. Other, fireless, creatures also have achieved the Mind, but like us, there is merely a collection of individuals. The way humans burn calories in the head is natural miracle. It doesn't predicate good or evil, oddly enough, only exacerbating whatever motive exists.

As our brains grew and our thoughts gestalted, innovation often manifested materially, in an ever-growing technological revolution. Artifacts testify to the increasing complexity of human industry. From two-sticks to rockets, and rocks to computers...Lascaux Cave to the Cistine Cieling...Hadrian's Wall to Operation Desert Storm...cauterization to genetic engineering....

Altamira cave,Spain

Fire helps humans in ecological control. It is no wonder that there is a perception that *man was given dominion* over

105

the earth. At first we mimicked Nature, only later cravenly caving to our own desires and devices to advance in ever greater rates on the uncivilized world. Regardless of the "Man Against Nature"  theme so prevalent in historical and modern culture, and although there is no inherent evil or danger in Nature towards humans–no moreso than for any other life-form–we insist upon *never* returning to the Wild without sure-fire! If, by accident, we find ourselves thus...fire is always proposed as one of the first efforts towards survival.

With fire we can tackle great trees, overwhelm great herds, select for plants and animals, revitalize entire tracts, fertilize one plot. Fire clears pathways and prepares the way for food production–passive *and* intensive. Hunts are made much more successful through fire, be the influence in strategy or weapon industry or preservation.

Fire's light has become the human security blanket–well I suppose it always has been via Sol. Our torches help share fire's wealth, leading us into territories never before open to our kind. As we use fire around the cookhearth for cuisine and industry–steaming, roasting, baking, charring, cracking, parching, smoking, smudging, coloring, blackening, burning–we laugh over the flames at the other smiling faces while we straighten shafts, bend wood, make or soften glues, treat stone, burn bowls, dig out canoes, finish pelts and hides, fire clay, scorch shell, preserve wood and food, sharpen and harden sticks, crush pigments, smelt and smith, clean, heal, repel, communicate, heat, light, ritualize and in general alter our state. It is thus. Fire inspires us, guides us, leads us, nurtures us, metes out punishments and restores us.

> By day God led them by a pillar of smoke, by night
> a pillar of fire for light. This Way they traveled day or night.
> Never did the pillar of smoke or fire leave its place ahead of
> the People.
>
> Exodus 14:21

The very act of "drilling" up a fire is tribute to fire as a *processual foundational technology.* Configuring mechanical devices—however simple—to generate an ember at record speeds as short as 5 seconds...this is a marvel. Imagine the improvement in using this selfsame device with a stone drill bit to process hard shell! Suddenly *everyone* can "afford" one of those lovely shell necklaces! Granted, bow drilling is still exercise—as you will find out—but so much an improvement over mere hand drilling. Of course the pump-drill is likely based on the to and fro elements embodied in the bow-drill or the "strap" modified hand-drill. The force is lighter, more delicate. Bow drilling is brute power to the pump-drill's precise-ness. Keeping in mind that the pump-drill is essentially an inferior technique for generating fire, it is a delightful technology owing existence to the human dimension of fire, and lending a mental gestalt—the flywheel—back into the Fire Revolution matrix. In the next chapter you'll also read about the fire-piston, an ingenious contraption that challenges mastery, but revolutionizes human thought. Through fire technologies like the fire-piston the applications of fire expanded into our concepts of machinery and electronics, indeed literally the *science* of our modern worldview and cosmology.

Truly said, and clearly evident, fire is man's best friend. It can also bring out the worst enemy in ourselves. To conclude this brief discussion of fire as a human foundational technology, consider how the multi-layer dynamic of human culture is expressed with fire in the core:

Cooking silicas goes back thousands of years. But after we heat treated flints and cherts, we made our *own* "obsidian." Silica in extreme heat becomes glass, with fresh flaked edges up to 500 times sharper than any metal scalpel used in modern surgery. Nevertheless, the laser is sharper still!

Beyond silicas, we have long been 'firing' ceramics—Jars of Clay whose kaolin (itself a hydrous aluminum silicate) usually mixed with some additive like sand or shell—to make pottery cooking and storage containers. When greenware is slowly exposed to the Curie Temperature, ferrous ions (and others!) are re-arranged and will never again return to their previous state. They are 'fired.' It is a blessing to modern archaeology—and to the passion for the historical perspective—that fire is so ubiquitous. Without fire many archaeological remains would not be preserved. Even *within* archaeological *interpretation* we can see the convoluted inter-relationship sponsored by fire. Pottery commonly has decoration, and one of the most frequent in southeastern American archaeology is the *water* symbol. Isn't it ironic that when hydrogen (the most basic and common element in the Universe) is oxidized, the by-products are energy...and water.

Art, music, dance, cuisine, architecture, travel, trade, ritual, religion, spirituality, medicine, literature, science...layer after layer...culture after culture...time after time *fire* is at the *heart* of the *matter*.

# Other Ways

"I am human. Nothing human can be alien to me."
                              —Terance, 5th Century B.C.


**There** are many "primitive" ways to make fire. Each is special in its own way, with peculiar challenges and rewards. As you encounter each one, your mind is gently re-minded of the loveliness of thought. And feeling! The exhultation expressed within our souls as we accomplish something so...mundane...and yet so...primal. I can honestly say that each fire moves me. I must also say that every student of mine who achieves fire comes away renewed. This is inviolate. You will not be an exception. It appears, after witnessing years of friction fires, that anyone interested enough to learn, do and share their fire experience will be changed forever. Try it.

As far as I know, the remaining "primitive" fire techniques include the fire-plow, -saw, -string, -piston, and pump-drill. There also is iron pyrite/chert. I would consider it joyful to encounter another one. I hope that happens! I have succeeded in but not mastered the fire-plow, -saw, and -piston. Flint and steel is simple, but stepping back to iron pyrite has its own difficulties. They are close, but not exactly the same.

Keep in mind the fun modification of the bow-drill–and though *I don't remember* ever seeing or hearing of anyone else doing this, I can scarcely believe that my friends Jesse and Alexa Ihns and I were the first to do it!– wherein two or more people can drop the bow from the set and simply use the string 'twixt the hands. If you are alone, this is a greater challenge than using the bow. Reason: you still need the pressure block. What do you use to hold down the spindle? Your mouth? A large lean-to (trap-like) rock, or log? (I've heard it said...) Your knee? Whatever!

Tandem method

But if you have two or three people then fire is a fun game...especially for youth! It is just honest to say that recycling Universal Fire in primitive mechanical processes is physically, emotionally, intellectually and temporally taxing. So whenever fire-making is made accessible to youth (in safe manners) deep education occurs. My friends thoroughly enjoy the challenges in congenial pyromania. Pulling the string back and forth between two youth with another adding spindle stability and pressure is an easy way to approach combustion release temperatures. Fire is not inherently egocentric...so don't make it that way. Share your burdens and lend each other a helping hand.

In the opening chapter I relayed an original story that asserts my belief that the fire-plow may be the most ancient of human controlled fire generation techniques. My reasons are simply stated: grinding seems to me more basic than either bashing or drilling. Drilling is clever, bashing (flintknapping) is scientific. Grinding is a grueling and begrudging pasttime. Truly primitive. I can imagine an ancestor–so dimly distant–noticing the hardening quality of stick grinding on dead tree trunk, making a tougher digging and gouging tool. Time after time that elusive, fearful, mouth-watering scent of smoke tempted nostril after nostril and it was only a matter of time before a particularly adept *Homo*-grinder toolmaker was involved in a particularly unique manifestation of quantum mechanics and poof!, fire.

Regardless of the question of which technique is the "most ancient"–as if we could assert for certain–the age-old manner imbedded in each method remains codified. The fire-plow, for instance, utilizes a typically harder wood as the "plow" and a softer wood as the "hearth." The plow needs to be whittled to a somewhat tapered "point," though edge would be the more appropriate word. As the plow is moved to and fro a groove is ground and charred. Ideally–and practice *really* helps make a difference here–each stroke would stop *just slightly short* of the previous strokes' stopping point, not jarring the accumulated dust pile from its comfortable seat. This is rather important in the -plow method, as the insular element of a growing dust pile is *crucial* in allowing the temperature to rise to combustion release. Unlike the so-exactly focused friction in the drilling methods, plowing requires a significant focused determination and awareness of movement and situation. Once ember ignition occurs, attaining flame in a tinder bundle remains the same. Success in the fire-plow method often entails a more "brute-force" effort, but honestly I believe that *every* fire generating method is improved when the practitioner dwells on style, skill and elegance, instead of merely raw strength. I really can't emphasize this enough. Please take it to heart. ( see **Fig.1**; Fire-plow )

The fire-string or -thong is another rudimentary fire starting technique. A "hearthboard" of a softer wood (cedar, basswood, etc) is split lengthwise (but not necessarily completely in half) to allow a string to pass under the upper piece. The string moves back and forth "under" the notched wood, but "over" a small tinder bundle "pinched" in the "split." The tinder bundle collects the growing dust as the string grinds away at the hearth. If all goes well, the temperature reaches combustion release and the dust ignites, already in the tinder. Obviously, non-vegetative cord is inferior for this method, as hide, gut, sinew or hair tends to "melt," not burn. Just as obviously, a string with low tensile strength will merely cause frustration. A person is well advised to pursue the strongest cord available, from vegetable sources: dogbane, yucca, hemp, flax, etc. I am under the impression that there are some modifications extant of the basic system described here, primarily with regards to the "split" wood and "notch" concepts. Experiment! ( see **Fig. 2**; Fire-string )

Making an ember with the fire-saw process is great fun, but my experiences indicate that the -saw is a somewhat exclusionary method with regards to materials. My successes have *only* been with bamboo. I assume that there are other materials that will work–and although I've tried rivercane, and believe it should succeed, I have not yet met with cane fire. It is certainly possible to spend *lots* of time preparing materials to suit the constraints of the method–concave and convex parts, etc.–but why spend that kind of time modifying materials best used in another fire building method? But to each their own, so please feel free to carve away and make a fire-saw kit from whatever materials you want. If you decide to stick with hollow reed type materials, be especially cognizant of the sharp edged qualities as you split out the blanks. Grasses (and bamboo and rivercane are large grasses) have a fair amount of silica in them, and their structure is such that you can be easily cut. Grass cuts burn, too, believe me. There is a balance and skill in stabilizing the "bottom" piece of bamboo between your waist and the ground, as well as in gently holding the tinder in place over the grooved notch being sawn as an ember is pursued. ( see **Fig. 3**; Fire-saw )

In the mid 19th century explorers and anthropologists documented the fire-piston being used by many Asian cultures. The -piston is a compression technique, wherein a combustible material (usually something pre-charred, like a fungus or shredded bark, or crushed charcoal) is inserted into a shallow concavity at the tip end of a "piston." The piston has a "gasket" (thin string) which helps seal the diameter of the piston snugly into the "chamber." Bamboo is, again, a common material for the fire-piston, but by no means the only one. I've seen plexiglas, mahogany, oak, hickory, cane, horn, antler pistons, among others. The plexiglas is particularly intriguing, as you can witness the "spark" if you perform the technique in the dark! The piston is gently inserted into the chamber, and then with extreme force plunged fully to the bottom. The essential finish is to rapidly remove the plunger allowing the ember oxygen, hence remaining alive. It is often held forth that this technique is the antiquated precursor to the internal combustion engine, and I acknowledge the sense in such an assumption. ( see **Fig. 4**; Fire-piston )

Pump-drills are not really designed to make fire, rather to drill holes. Human industry in things like shell carving, jewelry, architechture, musical instruments and many others have been advanced by the relative ease of hole carving with a pump-drill. Using gravity, momentum, inertia and mass interacting in a flywheel, downward pressure is attained as is the all important re-

charge of the device. A pump-drill is composed of a spindle shaft, cross-bar, cord, flywheel and drill chucks. The drill might be a stone point, or a yucca (or some other combustible) plug. Pump-drills designed to create fire are larger than most practical drills for day to day primitive manufacturing. Large pump-drills are very fun, however, and it is simply amazing to see how fast a stone point will blast through a plank of hard-wood that was split using only wooden, antler, or stone wedges with a primitive maul. Ancient lifeways do *not* imply incompetent lifeways! ( see **Fig.5**; Pump-drill )

As far as flint and steel goes, percussive fire starting tech-niques seem to appear around 5,000 years ago, in Europe. One could assume that people crunched rocks together all over the place, though. Bashing two pieces of iron pyrite together, or smashing an edge of flint or chert onto the iron pyrite, has been proposed by Ken Wee as a "not very effective" fire technology. Processed steel (forged) struck with chert is *very* effective. Either way, the spark is so short lived that it is necessary to provide a coal extender to fuel the jumped spark . Today's common mate-rial is "charred cloth." Using a metal "box" with a small hole punched in the top, cook pure cotton or some other vegetable fabric/material until no more smoke issues forth from the orifice. When the smoke stops, remove the tin from the coals and let it cool completely. Upon opening, find the blackened, charred remains which will catch and hold a live spark, to transfer to tinder. In ancient times, prior to Altoid boxes, other materials were likely used to catch the spark, including certain of the *Polyporaceae* fungus family. Iron pyrite and flints have been found in neolithic graves, suggestive of their importance for either survival or ritual, among others. A spark produced in this manner is—in actuality—a tiny bit of metallic mineral super-heated to combustion by the concussive force. Oetzi, "The Iceman," is around 5,300 years old. In his accoutrements were found high quality flints with pyrite particulates imbedded. Also in his kit: *fomes* tinder fungus.

Oetzi's Kit
(ca. 5,300 years B.P.)

Birch bark container to carry coal.

Flint dagger with woven bark sheath

Pressure flaker, lime wood handle with stag antler tip.

Flint flakes and scraper

Polypore tinder fungus, strung on belt

Iron pyrite (found embedded in the flint from percussion)

Bone awl

Touchwood

In any fire building process, it is essential that a spark or ember is combusted, maintained and enkindled into flame. No method spontaneous creates flame from nothing, not even chemical reactions. There is *always* the spark. Once an ember is inculcated, it is possible to use a primitive "match" to create flame. The late 18th century saw the first rudimentary matches, with their use spreading fairly rapidly. The first true match was "invented" in 1824 by John Walker, who used potassium chlorate, sulfur and gum arabic on the end of a stick. Friction sparked an enflamed reaction. Just sulfur and binder "matches" can also be used to "touch-off" an ember already produced by friction.

*Figure 1*

# Fire-Plow

- One of the few methods where "brute" can be helpful.

- Style is more important than strength.

- Experiment with ALL TYPES of woods, shrubs, and weeds.

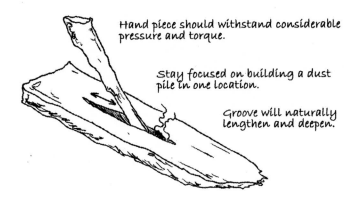

Hand piece should withstand considerable pressure and torque.

Stay focused on building a dust pile in one location.

Groove will naturally lengthen and deepen.

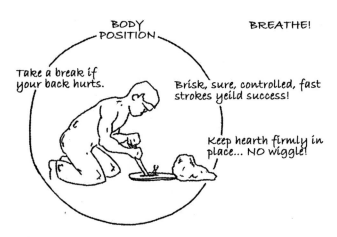

BODY POSITION

BREATHE!

Take a break if your back hurts.

Brisk, sure, controlled, fast strokes yeild success!

Keep hearth firmly in place... NO wiggle!

Figure 2

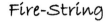

# Fire-String

- Use the strongest cord (multi-ply string) possible... ONLY VEGETATIVE!

- Use narrow sticks or splinters from broken limbs for the hearth.

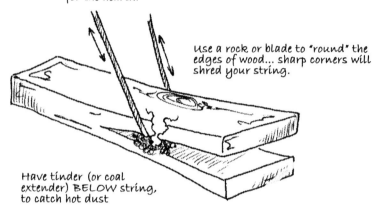

Use a rock or blade to "round" the edges of wood... sharp corners will shred your string.

Have tinder (or coal extender) BELOW string, to catch hot dust

BODY POSITION

BREATHE!

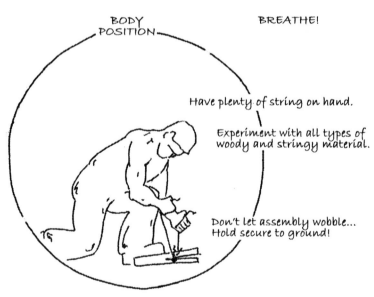

Have plenty of string on hand.

Experiment with all types of woody and stringy material.

Don't let assembly wobble... Hold secure to ground!

Figure 3

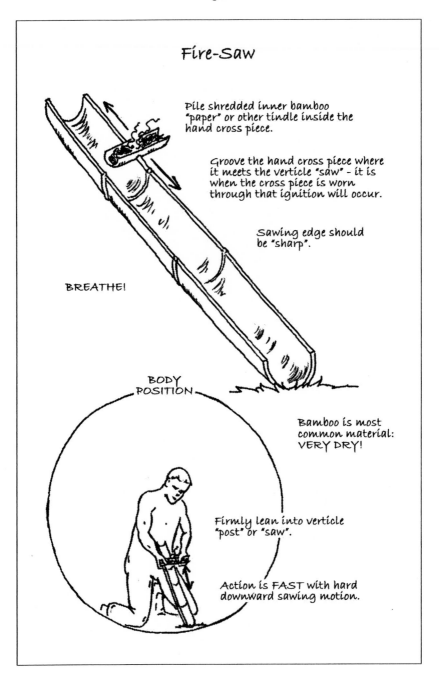

# Fire-Saw

Pile shredded inner bamboo "paper" or other tindle inside the hand cross piece.

Groove the hand cross piece where it meets the verticle "saw" - it is when the cross piece is worn through that ignition will occur.

Sawing edge should be "sharp".

BREATHE!

BODY POSITION

Bamboo is most common material: VERY DRY!

Firmly lean into verticle "post" or "saw".

Action is FAST with hard downward sawing motion.

Figure 4

# Fire-Piston

- Transfer spark with coal extender from piston tip to tindle.

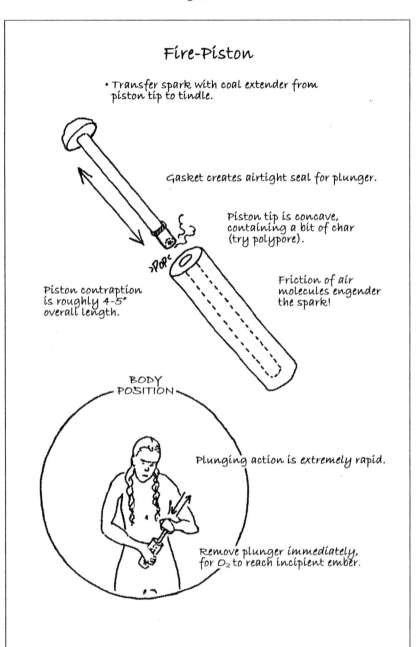

Gasket creates airtight seal for plunger.

Piston tip is concave, containing a bit of char (try polypore).

Piston contraption is roughly 4-5" overall length.

Friction of air molecules engender the spark!

BODY POSITION

Plunging action is extremely rapid.

Remove plunger immediately, for $O_2$ to reach incipient ember.

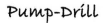

Figure 5

## Pump-Drill

- Large pump-drills are needed for fire making, smaller drills are sufficient for beads and such.

- To effect the proper (and faster and faster) "re-charge" of the fly wheel assembly, practice slowly at first.

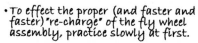

Each time you depress the pump- finish by lessening up on the cross handle.

Fly wheel MUST be perfectly centered by mass... weight symmetry is key!

Drill "chucks" can be woody plugs for fire, or bi-polar triangle bits of stone, hafted to a compression fitting which inserts into the concave (or hollow) distal tip.

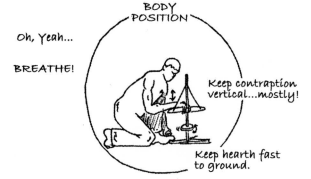

BODY POSITION

Oh, Yeah...

BREATHE!

Keep contraption vertical...mostly!

Keep hearth fast to ground.

# Sustaining Fire

"For the first time in the history of man, the planet he inhabits is encompassed by a single global civilization... [T]his makes the modern world an essentially dramatic place, with so many peoples in so many places resisting coexistence with each other. And yet its only chance for survival is precisely such coexistence."

—President Vaclav Havel, Czech Republic

When I was a young boy I heard my father say, "He who cuts his own wood warms himself twice." Of course at first I assumed that clever euphemistic phrase encouraging my work ethic *belonged* to my dad. Now I'm sure that elders have been exhorting (extorting?) their subordinates to ever greater yields and achievements, for any number of reasons, forever. Perhaps you can appreciate the subtle humor I've discovered in my own life as I've developed my pyrotechnic skills, with respect to my father's quip? Now, a camping trip offers not so much as chores to be checked off, but opportunities for experimentation. Experiential learning pays off. Creating a safe hearth, with emergency awareness and first-response convenient, has become a meaningful lesson every time I am tending fire around more youthful or inexperienced individuals. Knowing what fuel to gather (avoid poisonous plants!) for light, heat or longevity, respectively, is an important thing. Botany is such a necessary knowledge for the fire-maker.

By now you have—hopefully—had the eminent (and imma-nent) experience of exerting fire. Perhaps you'd like to explore some of the many uses of fire discussed thus far? That means, of course, that you must understand the needs of your fire. First,

please control your fire. Be respectful and mindful of the embodiment of Gaia. You are an important part, but not anointed with omnis-cience. Nurture the life around

you, and in return that life will continue to nurture you. Keep in mind that Universal Reality deems all Existence, and although your current life will surrender to the death experience one day, right now you are given endless opportunities to grow and wor-ship the Almighty. Spirit will guide you, but you must learn to lis-ten in every way, irreducibly sensing the presence of Immanence. Ritualized supplication such as quietly drilling a fire for compan-ionship through the dark night is an immane element giving defi-nition to our condition, insight into our collective consciousness, celebration of our humanity...for all of our feats and foibles. We truly *are* One.

And how to keep that fire *alive*? A question metaphori-cally asked by every single one of us, so many times! I am not confident of my abilities as a lover, worker, inventor, writer or marriage counselor, so I'll limit my discussion to keeping the hearth aflame.

Always treat fire with respect. If you ignore it it will either go out or go out of control. Either is a very bad thing. You need to figure this out, clearly and decisively, okay? Do *not* mistreat fire. Do not *misuse* fire.

> Consider what a great forest is set on fire by a tiny spark. The tongue also is a fire, a world of evil among the parts of the body. It can corrupt a whole body, setting the whole course of a life on fire...itself set on fire by hell.
>
> James 3: 5&6

King Prasenajit of Kosala is purported to have said to the 38 year-old Buddha: "Reverend, you are young and yet are called the 'Enlightened One.' There are holy men eighty, ninety years old who do not make such claims! How can you?" The Buddha replied: "It is not a matter of age. A tiny spark can destroy a city. A baby poisonous snake can kill as easy as its parent. The young prince can become a king. And me? Surely any young monk might have enlightenment and change the world."

Keep your fire out of wet weather. Elevate it if you are camped—unfortunately—on soggy ground. If the terrain allows for it, and you are ensconced for a while, go ahead and dig a pit for your fire...and there are any number of pit features represented in archaeology and documented by anthropology. Be creative. A pit is of value in conserving radiant heat longer, in that energy is not lost to entropy. You do not lose cooking surfaces; as a matter of fact, a well designed earth-oven is a beautiful and complex system. Earth-ovens conserve fuel, heat, maximize utility all the while encouraging safety. ( see **Fig. 6**; Earth oven)

*Banking* a fire encourages a live coal upon demand. Usually a fire is banked at bedtime, with hopes that an ember lives on the morrow. To bank a fire, it is a good idea to set a good bed

Figure 6

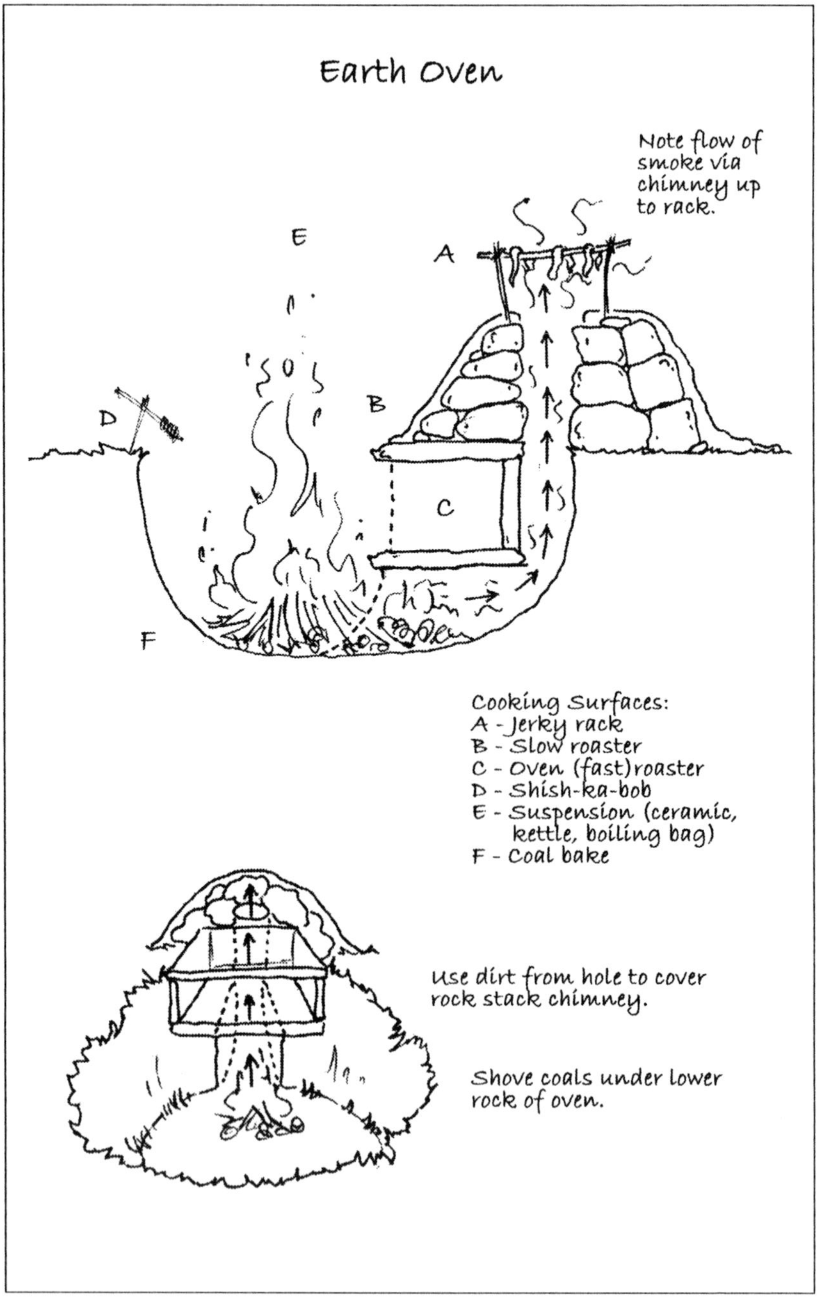

# Earth Oven

Note flow of smoke via chimney up to rack.

E

A

B

D

C

F

Cooking Surfaces:
A - Jerky rack
B - Slow roaster
C - Oven (fast) roaster
D - Shish-ka-bob
E - Suspension (ceramic, kettle, boiling bag)
F - Coal bake

Use dirt from hole to cover rock stack chimney.

Shove coals under lower rock of oven.

of hardwood coals to recieve a large log. The log should be backed up against a wall of the pit, or a hearth rock, allowing only one side to be readily exposed to air. Some people use spent ashes or rocks to "cover" the coals spilling out from under the banked log. Regardless of individual idiosyncracies, the process should slow the consumption rate of fuel, with the intent of having a live coal to re-kindle. In this manner, it is without doubt that our ancestors were able to keep a fire going for days, weeks, months or even years.

Keeping a tindle, coal extender, and heart-pine handy to the hearth is a good idea. But please take the time to educate others in proper fire etiquette. No one likes a smoky fire unless they are: jerking meat, finishing a hide, purifying themselves or trying to communicate. Keep the smoke down by learning how and when to feed your fire. Avoid using leaves, in general, although a few judicious dry leaves at the very beginning is alright. It is a nasty calamity when some ignorant puts your fat-lighter pine on the fire underneath your cooking deer tenderloin. Blah.

Also, don't get all worked up by sensationalism. For example, foods do *not*–truly–garner the flavor of a particular *type* of smoke (i.e. hickory) *unless* they've been in that smoke for around two hours or more. Jerking meat, by the way, is not at all about cooking the meat. Rather, when meat is jerked the smoke prevents flies from "blowing" the meat (ever wondered why "blowing it" can mean "ruining it?") by laying their maggoting eggs. If flies are kept clear, then the meat can air dry. The smoke acts as preservative, flavoring and lends its low heat to the drying speed. Keep in mind that almost all bacteria and creatures die when exposed to temperatures associated with direct flame, if the heat is sustained long enough. So even if meat is rotten, it can be cooked and eaten...carefully. It still doesn't mean it will taste good or be a particularly safe choice. You should plan well enough to never have to eat rotten meat–as Chris McCandless sadly discovered. Jerking meat is much more pleasant.

Preparedness is a good thing. Collect all of your tools, materials, fuels, etc. well in advance of when you think you'll need them. Rushing around in the dark for wood is onerous. Learn how to find tiny, *eentsy-beensy* (pardon that, but people really have never taken me seriously when I tell them that we need *small twigs!*) branches for the infancy of your fire. A couple of handfuls of small fuel really helps ensure the life of a new fire. Upsize to "logs" slowly. Don't think you *need* perfectly chopped firewood, either. The Creek Indians (and most others) regularly operated

what they called a "star-fire," wherein long dry logs and branches are collected upon arriving at a campsite and fuel is added radially from each direction into the fire. Each limb or branch is disassembled as far as possible by breaking with hands, knees, feet, rocks or torqued between two trees. Once a sizable stack of variable diameter sticks and logs is collected–none being much longer than six feet

or so–the fire is enkindled. Very efficient.

Gloves and/or a pair of fire-tongs are great for rummaging near high heat. It is a good idea to assign at least one person to be primarily responsible for the fire...for safety, maintenance, procreation, use, etc. Fire is very dangerous, and children should be properly educated to safe attendance while in its proximity.

Fire charred wood scrapes much easier–handy if you are practicing primitive with stone tools. Baked wood, sanded, smoothed, oiled, used...is a beautiful thing. Digging sticks, bowls, boxes, canoes–any number of woodcrafts are indebted to fire. If you take the pitchy rosin of pine and other trees–experiment!–and melt it, admixturing waxes, oils, crushed dung and/or other resins; finally combining in small amounts of powdered charcoal you get a compound. This is an essentially waterproof glue that, although it can be brittle with too much charcoal, is very effective and useful. Hide glue is made by boil-

ing down animal scraps–hooves, bones, hide, hair, 'parts' (though all have other uses)–until the collagen is released into water suspension. After cooling, the congealed collagen on the surface is removed, rendered again if necessary, thinly sliced and dried. It is reconstituted by powdering and moistening.

Pine pitch glue sticks

Try a gypsy meal sometime, where you wrap a bunch of foodstuffs inside edible leaves and plaster clay all over it. Slowly roll it into the coals, letting ashes and charcoal kind of intercalate into the coating. When you get the roll into the coals, give it a few minutes until your judgement–or hunger–takes precedence. You'll need to experiment. Think of it as adding to the archaeological record. If you have a watertight wooden or woven container ( or even a rawhide 'bucket') you can heat egg shaped rocks in the coals, and then drop them into the container of water. Make soups, stews, teas and so on without risking the integrity of your cooking container.

Old pottery (and other oxidized ferrous-containing substances) can be ground–along with charcoal–into paints. Binders (heading towards glues) like plant-saps are prepared by boiling them down, thickening like maple syrup.

Fire can be propagated into primitive candles and torches to extend the life of the fire, or to increase the range of light. Ceramic or stone bowls work great for primitive candles. Rendered animal fats serve as the fuel (with a low melting point, a bowl of fat is liquified by a burning wick pretty quick), while vegetable fluff (cattail, finely shredded cedar bark, etc.) is a tufted wick. Different wicks burn at different rates, so experiment with your local materials. Torches can be simple or compound; pine knots make a quick and quick-burning torch. Or you can collect barks, fluffs, pine pitch and so forth to construct a more complicated and longer burning affair. Either way, when using torches be aware of hot torch particulates in desuetudinal descent. Ouch. Especially in the hair!

Long match ingredients.

Sometimes when a group of practicing primitives is on the move, a fire is toted along. While I have watched a freshly drilled ember smoulder unaided for eight minutes or more (big coal, much dust), and have extended an embers life with polypore and such for well over two hours in a punk-pot...it is feasible and rudimentary to store a coal from a fire and travel with it for over ten hours and successfully re-kindle a flame. Using similar principles espoused throughout this volume, identify the best smouldering agents and shreddable barks and fluffs in the local environs. Construct your "long-match" by packing the finest mix in the center of your tube shaped bundle, with ever rougher textures to the exterior. Finish by wrapping coarse bark strips snugly around the entire ensemble. To use simply expose the innards at one end, inserting a thumb-sized coal into the body of the match. Pull the coverings back around the coal, and occasionally check for continuous heat radiating from the

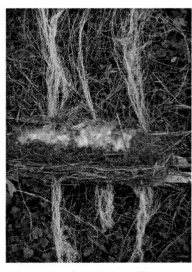

Long match innards, roll it up...

bundle as the match slowly degrades. Avoid too much air flow. A similar process can be achieved using a punk-pot. Any non-flammable container can be stuffed with smouldering agents and used to carry a coal. Finally, and this tip is great for flint/steel kits, if you use a combination of coal extender/charred material inside a "tube" of bark or cane, a spark will often catch on the exposed "wick" and stay lit long enough to, say, light a pipe.

...Smokin'!

# Long Match

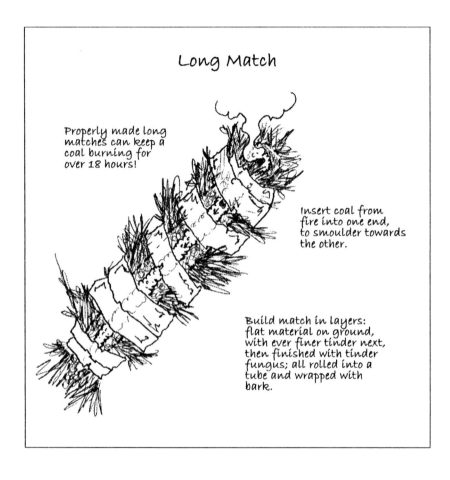

Properly made long matches can keep a coal burning for over 18 hours!

Insert coal from fire into one end, to smoulder towards the other.

Build match in layers: flat material on ground, with ever finer tinder next, then finished with tinder fungus; all rolled into a tube and wrapped with bark.

# Fire Spirit

"For, after all, what is man in nature? A nothing compared with infinity, all when compared with nothing. A middle point between nothing and all. Infinitely far from understanding the extremes...equally incapable of seeing the nothing when he emerges and the infinity in which he is engulfed."
                                                                    –Blaise Pascal


**Fire.** Dynamic, pure, illimitable life. Firstborn of Our Universe. Law enforcer. Destroyer, healer. Resurrection and Life. Conjunction of finite and infinite. Terrible beauty, sheer radiance. Expression of the infernal conflict between Good and Evil. Redeemer.

When we are *impassioned*, we find ourselves overcome with burning intensity for joy, fear, grief, hate, love. Passion may also be sublime desire or caustic agony. Humans–as in all of life–are begotten of fire. The gray matter of our brains and the thoughts of our minds...the science of our intellects...our desires, hopes, dreams...our conflicts and accords...the cornerstone of the temple of technology...the energy units we call calories which fuel the internal combustion of our bodies...all of it, given or influenced by fire. Fire animates the cosmos, and a crucible is its Source. It is no wonder that God's Voice emanates therein.

Not only is Existence predicated upon the innate procreative power of fire, but also is our ability to cognize Existence.

From the beginnings of Our Kind–those who fatefully chose to gather, nurture and use fire–we have become ever more aware. Our perspective and understanding of the seen and the unseen have been delineated by fire. Garnering more efficiency from our expenditure of time–a finite resource–our use of fire opened portals and pathways not available to other animals. "Doorways" as simple as torchlight leading into the bowels of the earth, or as penetrative as the heat-activation of pyschoactive substances.

If it weren't for fire, we would never have sailed–for without water to sail upon and thermal generated winds to escort us, to what use would the billowing sails (whose fibers were grown in fire based agriculture) and hand-hewn planks (whose wood was harvested and finished by tools created in the fiery forge) sealed with pitch and turpentine (processed and fabricated via extreme heat, mixed with powdered charcoal) be? Without the burning stars could we have learned to navigate? Planes, trains and automobiles and of course space-ships all owe their existence to fire.

You see, fire allowed for agriculture, hunting and animal husbandry, preservation and conservation. Fire's efficiency gave us *time*. Time to whistle at birds and find music. Time to carve or sculpt an artistic gift exchanging the spark of romance. Time to play games. Time to heal. Time to plot and plan. Time to reflect–staring deeply into the ephemerally pulsing rainbow-heart of flame–on why we are here.

In the friendliness of firelight we confronted our fears. Basking in the warm glow of embers we explored love, engendering new life and intuitively redefining our very motives.

Fire gave birth to our science–our *knowing*. I guess we'll never know for sure "how" or "what" we *knew* before the Fall into sentience promulgated by the human dimension of fire. Clearly, all we know now is owed to fire. I hold it self-evident that human gnosis—be it scientific or religious—originates in fire, from quantum to confusion. Omniscience was not given to Us. We simply accept this Ultimate Reality. It is our place to do so. The gift of fire—for surely that is what the most powerful lifeforce in the Known Universe must be—has been given to humanity. (It is also the only known entity to overwhelm gravity) And this gift is ours to use as we see fit.

The parsimonious nature of this gift allows for our errors to be as they are, *and* furthermore offers assistance to those who would grow ever more aware. And like all gifts, to ignore any element contained within it is to reject the Spirit in which it was given.

For the gift-giver, implicit in the giving is a desire to be better known, appreciated, respected, honored and loved. And fire is a gift from our Maker. Being mindful that it is God's Will that We Are, try and reciprocate. Can we not acknowledge that our existence accrues not from our willfulness, rather that our willfulness is a reaction to our existence? A person's beliefs express their will, and their will is their own. We each have the right to serve as role models to assist in the development of the ultimate movement of will: to be aware of, submit to, and find joy in the fact that the Maker's Will will always infinitely encompass our own.

# Desperate

## Wild Fire

I am open
No other way to be
Any attempt otherwise
Is killing me

Sweet voice
Are you you or me?
The origin in my thoughts
An endless sea
Of change

My God!

Constant as fate
Inevitable as destiny
Fickle as gravity
Torpid as fire
Responsive as water
Visible as wind
Consuming as desire

Dear God

Where is this 'God' that was promised? From the time of our ancestors *all is as it has been since Creation.* But do not forget that it was the Word of God that bespoke Creation; from water and destroyed by water; from fire and destroyed by fire, being reserved thus for judgment of the Unbelievers. A reminder, *'oh wise ones':* what is a second or a billion years to God? God is not slovenly nor forgetful; merely loving and nurturing of your love. But–like a thief–[your] Eternal Moment *will* come, roaring the heavens away and cremating elements...earth will be laid bare.

2 Peter 3: 4-10

The magnetization ratio of a paramagnetic substance to its magnetizing force is inversely proportionate to absolute temperature. Just keep that in mind.

...and sleep close to the fire.

# Selected Glossary and Random Thoughts

**anthropology**–n. the study of humankind

**archaeology**–n. scientific study of ancient human lifeways

**art**–n. creative work which imitates, supplements, alters or counteracts the work of nature in a manner that affects the sense of beauty

**bow**–n. anything curved or bent

**bow-drill**– a mechanical device for generating a fire ember or hole, relying on a bow, spindle, hearthboard, and pressure block as descriptive components

**brain-tan**–n. animal hide softened for use with a treatment of brains and usually smoke

**carbon**–n. non-metallic chemical element with atomic wt. 12.01115, at no. 6, found in many inorganic and all organic compounds

**chain reaction**–a self-sustaining series of chemical or nuclear reactions in which the products of the reaction contribute directly to the propagation of the process

**coal**–n. (in our context) an ember; a piece of glowing or charred wood, coal or similar substance

**coal extender**–any of a number of organic substances which readily smoulder and extend the life of an ember; i.e. cattail and thistle fluff, charred cloth, certain types of polypore mushroom and fuzzy leaves, etc.

**combustion**–n. oxidation resulting in heat and light; the act or process of burning

**cordage**–n. cords and ropes, collectively

**craft**–n. & v. skill, proficiency; a trade requiring manual dexterity or skilled artistry; to make by hand

**Curie Temperature (Point)**–the temperature at which ferro-magnetic ions precess to a paramagnetic state, usually before the melting of the substance

**death**–n. the apparent cessation of animated life within a body

**earthskills**–experiential archaeology; the theoretical study and praxis of ancient lifeways; the primitive interaction of humans within their ecosystem

**electric**–adj. of, charged by, or conveying electricity

**electricity**–n. a fundamental property of all particles in matter; electrons and positrons have an associated force field that can be separated by an expenditure of energy; such an electrical charge can be induced by friction, chemicals or force-field differentials, made manifest by the accumulation of electrons on an atom or body, thereby inculcating a negative charge in desuetude to a positive charge (gee, the River of Life?)

**electromagnetism**–magnetism induced by electric current

**ember**–incipient fire; a manifest coalescence of a chain reaction between heat, fuel and oxygen

**eternal**–without end

**fire**–n. a living entity manifesting transmogrification of mass via combustion into light, heat, gas and material particulates; purus

(Latin) (fire) dynamic, pure, illimitable life

**fireboard**–see hearthboard

**fire-cord**–antiquated method of generating an ember wherein a string rubbing against a base yields dust and combustion release temperatures

**fire-plow**–antiquated method of generating an ember wherein a tapered plow is grooved into a base generating dust and combustion release temperatures

**fire-piston**–antiquated fire generating technique wherein compressed air ignites a combustible material

**fire-saw**–antiquated fire generating process wherein a convex trough is sawn perpendicular to a sharp edge yielding dust and combustion release temperatures

**fission**– a splitting or breaking up into parts; the splitting of an atomic nucleus resulting in the release of large amounts of energy

**fusion**–popular music combining different styles (as jazz and rock); a union via or like melting–as a merging of diverse, distinct, or separate elements into a unified whole; the transmogrifying union of atomic nuclei forming heavier nuclei resulting in the transmutation of vast sums of energy with certain light elements as origin

**flintknapping**–the artful science of flaking siliceous stone to create tools

**floating (technique)**–a re-introduced method attributed to Scott Kuipers of hand-drilling an ember without ever removing the active hands from the drill

**Gaia**–n. the life-force of planet Earth; if bacteria in our digestive system are an element comprising what we are, then surely we are an element comprising Gaia

**gnosis**–intuitively knowing

**God**–spontaneous perfecting ultimate universal realization via creative eternal spirit of infinite sentience. That which makes, Is

**hand-drill**–antiquated method of generating an ember wherein a slender stalk is twirled between the hands into a hearthboard; likely one of the two most ancient human fire generating methods

**harbinger**–literally 'provider of lodging'; now colloquially something or someone who precedes with the intent of announcement

**hearth**–where a fire is kept; also conventionally used to refer to a home or family life

**hearthboard**–a small plank-like piece of wood (usually notched) where the drilling of a spindle yields charred dust or an ember

**hydrogen**–a flammable, colorless, odorless gasseous element symbolized by "H" with an atomic weight of 1.00797; atomic element One having a melting point of -259.14 and a boiling point of -252.8 degrees, Celsius; it is the Lightest of All

**inculcate**–to tread in, impress upon or persistently urge

**infinite**–beyond measure, incomprehensible; limitless, without beginning or end; (math) indefinitely large or immense, capable only of reflective one-to-one self-correspondence (infinite set); (The Infinite) God

**in-love**–an irrational state of overwhelming desire; or a sincere committed passion

**interstice**–n. the space between, esp. ephemeral space; a gap or break in something generally continuous, or a short space of time between events

**intrinsic**–true to the core nature of a thing; essence(s) dictated by inherency, not externalities

**life**–animation, vivacity, vigor; an illimitable property instilling animae to what might otherwise be inorganic, inactive or inanimate

**lightning**–to enlighten; to give off flashes of light; a discharge of electrical light energy momentarily connecting earth to clouds

**love**–see also in-love– an interest, fondness, goodwill, attraction, passion or desire

**mental gestalt**–a movement of intellect wherein paradigms dictating the integrated structure or pattern of experience or gnosis yield to spontaneity

**money**–standardized accounting units primarily used to define the fluctuating relationship between finite resources, labor and demand for services or products; arbitrary value denominationally emplaced upon effort or materials in order to control human behaviour

**Muscogee**–a distinct and ancient language family indigenously occupying the North American southeast at the time of European colonization circa 1600 A.D.; a reference to the many 'tribal' affiliations of the historic southeastern U.S. issuing from a common lingual stock, believed to be the pre-Columbian "Mississippians"

**nature**–the evolving sum total of the physical universe; the essential character of a thing

**oxygen**–colorless, odorless, tasteless gasseous element with atomic weight 15.9994; at number 8; it is essential to Life Forces. Oxidation with this most common element will engender the removal of electrons from an atom or ion–effectively increasing the positive or decreasing the negative valence therein

**phoenix**–a mythical fire-creature in bird-dragon shape which died flaming into ashes, to be reborn

**praxis**–practice, as distinguished from theory; i.e.–the doing, not the daydreaming

**pressure block**–a hand-held object (wood, antler, stone, bone, etc) stabilizing and pressuring the spindle of a friction fire kit

**primitive technology**–see also earthskills–ancient lifeways in praxis; field and labwork in Experimental Archaeology. Humans practicing archaic in an environment

**processual**–the course of being; continuing development; going in a process. Prepared by special treatment

**Prometheus**–[sic] pre-knowing, precognition, prescience, fore-sight (Greek) [in Greek myth] the titan demi-god responsible for procreating civilized humanity by the essential ingredient of fire, which he stole from Heaven. With a commuted sentence from liver eating vultures every day of his eternal life to living eternal-ly with Pandora, his exploits have been met with great success and tragic failure

**pyromaniac**–one who is engulfed by lurid fascination with fire

**Rule of Thirds**–safety guide to carving the hearthboard notch in a friction fire kit: from edge of charred depression, incise a notch comprising the center one-third of the circle, and entering into the hole approximately one-third to one-half the diameter

**science**–a 'way of knowing;' colloquially, a modern worldview making essential use of the so-called **"Scientific Method"**–incorporating reproduceable experiments–to verify, debunk or advance theory

**skill**–practiced capability; great ability in/and art, craft, or science. [archaic] "to make a difference"

**smoke**–vapors emanating from fire, basically comprised of ele-mental gasses, heat, and organic particulates

**soul**–summa persona en toto; the finish of a person in comple-tion

**spindle**–'dowel' held vertically and spun into a hearthboard to generate an ember–incipient fire; a lit coal used to ignite a tinder-bundle

**spirit**–essence; animative essential motivation inspiring (!) Life. Sentience not defined nor limited by the physic

**symbol**–a sign, image, character or object which makes refer-ence to or represents something else

**tinder bundle**–also called tindle –a 'birds-nest' arrangement of extremely finely shredded dry barks, grasses, leaves, certain mush-

147

rooms, etc. (tindling) to recieve an ember which will be oxygenated unto flame-age! Dude! You're getting a fire in your *dell* now!

**tool**–a device contrived to assist in completing a task

**transmogrify**–to change completely

**transmute**–to change from one form to another

**ubiquitous**–commonplace; appearing to be present everywhere at the same time, omnipresent

**universe**–our place of being; the cosmos and its nature

**vulcanism**–exploding forth (as in from) a volcano

**welcome mat**–a thin object used to collect dust in the hearth-notch while generating an ember, used to transfer the coal to tindle

**wylde**–well-intentioned nature

**Yeshua-mashiach**–[sic] the anointed (read: essentially blessed) liberation of God's assistance (Hebrew and Aramaic); founding will (logos–discourse) of the universe; common colloquially as "Jesus Christ" (Greek)

# References, further reading, so forth...

# = "ISBN"

**Archaeogeophysical Detection and Mapping of Chattooga Town Historic Site 38(oc)18, South Carolina** *by* Russell Cutts, University of Georgia Press, 1997

**Beyond Civilization: Humanity's Next Great Adventure** *by* Daniel Quinn. Three Rivers Press, 2000. #0609805363

**Bible, New International Version**. Tyndale House Publishers, 1997. #0842348921

**Blackbird Dreams** *by* Russell Cutts. The Wyldecraft Co., 2002. #0972683909

**Blue Mountain Buckskin** *by* Jim Riggs. Backcountry Publishing, reissue 2004. #0965867218

**Boy Scout Handbook** *by* BSA Staff. Applewood Books, 1997.

#1557094411

**A Brief History of Time** *by* Stephen Hawking. Bantam Books, 1998. #0553380168

**Bulletin of The Society of Primitive Technology** *by* David Wescott, Ed. Society of Primitive Technology, all issues.

**Coosa: The Rise and Fall of a Southeastern Mississippian Chiefdom** *by* Marvin Smith. Univ. of Florida Press, 2000. #0813018110

**Cosmos** *by* Carl Sagan. Ballantine Books, 1985. #0345331354

**Deerskins to Buckskins** *by* Matt Richards. Backcountry Publishing, 1997. #

**The Diversity of Life** *by* E.O. Wilson. W.W. Norton & Co., reissue 1999. #0393319407

**Earth Knack: Stone Age Living Skills** *by* Bart and Robin Blankenship. Gibbs Smith Publishers, 1996. #0879057335

**Essays** *by* Ralph Waldo Emerson. Perrenial Books, 1981. #0060909064

**From Lucy to Language** *by* Donald Johansen. and Blake Edgar. Simon and Schuster, 1996. #0684810239

**The Gnostic Gospels** *by* Elaine Pagel. Vintage Books, 1989. #0679724532
**A History of God** *by* Karen Armstrong. Ballantine Books, 1994.

#0345384563

**Iceman: Uncovering the Life and Times of a Prehistoric Man Found in an Alpine Glacier** by Brenda Fowler. Univ. of Chicago Press, 2001. #0226258238

**Indian Givers** by Jack Weatherford. Ballantine Books, 1988. #0449904962

**Into the Wild** by John Krakauer. Anchor Books, 1997. #0385486804

**Knights of Spain, Warriors of the Sun** by Charles Hudson. Univ. of Georgia Press, 1998. #0820320625

**The Qur'an (Oxford World Classics Hardcovers)** by M.A.S. Abdel Haleem. Oxford Univ. Press, 2004. #0192805487

**Living Buddha, Living Christ** by Thich Nhat Hanh. Riverhead Books, 1997. #1573225681

**Muhammed: A Biography of the Prophet** by Karen Armstrong. HarperSanFrancisco, 1993. #0062508865

**Ocmulgee Archaeology 1936-1986** by David Hally. Univ. of Georgia Press, 1994. #0820316067

**On the Duty of Civil Disobedience** by Henry David Thoreau. Signet Classics, reissue 1999. #0451527070

**Oxford History of Ancient Egypt** by Ian Shaw. Oxford Univ.

Press, 2002. #0192802933

**Primitive Technology–A Book of Earthskills** *by* David Wescott, Ed. Gibbs Smith Publishers, 1999. #0879059117

**Primitive Technology II–Ancestral Skills** *by* David Wescott, Ed. Gibbs Smith Publishers, 2001. #1586850989

**Primitive Wilderness Living and Survival Skills: Naked Into the Wilderness** *by* John and Geri McPherson. John McPherson, 1993. #0967877776

**Psychoanalysis of Fire** *by* Gaston Bachelard. Beacon Press, 1987. #0807064610

**Rich Mullins: Arrow Pointing to Heaven** *by* James Smith. Broadman and Holdman Publishers, 2002. #0805426353

**Son of Man: The Mystical Path to Christ** *by* Andrew Harvey. Putnam Publishing Group, 1999. #0874779928

**Southeastern Indians** *by* Charles Hudson. Univ. of Tennessee Press, 1978. #0870492489

**Steel Bonnets** *by* George MacDonald Fraser. Harpercollins Pub. Ltd., 1998. #0002727463

**Sun Circles and Human Hands** *by* Emma Lila Funderburk. Univ. of Alabama Press, reprint 2001. #0817310770

**Tao Te Ching** *by* LaoTsu, Gia Fu-Weng, Jane English. Vintage

Books, 1997. #0679776192

**101 Famous Poems** *by* Roy J. Cook, Ed.  McGraw-Hill Press, 1984. #0809288311

# ...and Related Websites

Neither the author nor the publisher claim responsibility for the content of these websites, but they seem fairly innocuous and in general fairly helpful. Websites in bold are the primary suggested starting points.

abotech.com
boss-inc.com
braintan.com
earth-connection.com
earthknack.com
**earthskills.net**
hollowtop.com
jackmountainbushcraft.com
motherearthnews.com
nols.edu
**primitive.org**
primitiveways.com
reinhardt.edu/funk
wilderness-survival.net
**wyldecraft.com**

# A Note on Plant Identification for Friction Fire

Okay, so by this point you might still harbor some resentment that I haven't given an exhaustive accounting of plants that yield fire in some form or fashion. I'm sorry about that. But this book is more about the making of the fire and the human relations therein. It is not intended to be a botanist's guide.

And anyway, if you haven't yet picked up that–technically–any wood can be used to generate fire due to the physical laws of the Universe (basically what you need to do is play with any local wood or plant matter that seems likely and see what works for you) well then I just don't know what to say. Can't you enjoy a little play time? Are you so dag-gone busy that you can't go for a walk?

But since there is a legitimate issue about "diminishing points of return" and the efforts we invest in our endeavors–and since I really do want everyone who reads this book to be able to make a friction fire as easily as possible–then I offer the following listing as a *decent* place to *start*. This list is intended to be *fairly* applicable from San Francisco to Savannah, Georgia, and from

Canada to Key West.  Good luck.  Be sparing.  God bless.

**Natives** (to N. America)

| | |
|---|---|
| Basswood, or American Linden | *Tilia americana* |
| Boxelder | *Acer negundo* |
| Cattail | *Typha latifolia* |
| Cedar | *Cedrus* and *Juniperus* spp. |
| Cottonwood | *Populus deltoides* |
| Cypress | *Taxodium distichum* |
| Elderberry | *Sambucus* spp. |
| Horseweed, Mare's Tail | *Conzya canadense* |
| Mule Fat | *Baccharus viminea* |
| Mullein | *Verbascum thapsis* |
| Sotol | *Dasylirion wheeleri* |
| Sycamore | *Plantanus occidentalis* |
| Tulip Tree, Poplar (Magnolia) | *Liriodendron tulipifera* |
| White Sage | *Alvia apiana* |
| Willow | *Salix* spp. |
| Yucca, spanish bayonet | *Yucca* spp. |

**Non-natives** (to N. America)

| | |
|---|---|
| Honeysuckle | *Lonicera japonica* |
| Kudzu | *Pueraria montana* var. *lobata* |
| Mimosa | *Albizia julibrissin* |
| Princess Tree, Royal Paulownia | *Paulownia tomentosa* |

Being "non-native" to North America, plan on cutting every single one of these dang plants, okay?  Burn them all up.  It's not that I'm hostile to these lifeforms, just their inappropriate invasion of native ecosystems.  Call me hypocritical if you want.

*A note on plant I.D.*

Cottonwood

Black Willow

Mullein

Basswood

## A cedar tree...

## ...and usefull parts

B–Bark

A–Dead branch

C–Peeling bark (tinder)

D–Needles

# Wild Fire

Cattails

Tulip Poplar bark

Tulip Poplar leaves

$TO$ the last there will be scoffers who take only their own counsel. These will be they who divide you, being selfish and base, without Spirit. You, however...you keep believing in your own way, and pray to the Holy Spirit. Love God mightily and yearn for a life eternally redeemed. Practice mercy for those who do doubt, sparing their being burned whenever possible; but be mindful why you are repulsed by them.

Jude 18-23

Printed in the United States
25356LVS00001B/184-384